SALVAGE STYLE IN YOUR HOME

Moira and Nicholas Hankinson

SALVAGE STYLE IN YOUR HOME

Moira and Nicholas Hankinson

Kyle Cathie Limited

First published in Great Britain 2000 by

Kyle Cathie Limited
122 Arlington Road
London NW1 7HP

general.enquiries@kyle-cathie.com

ISBN 1 85626 374 6

Text and designs © **Moira and Nicholas Hankinson**
Photography © **Tim Winter** except those listed below.

Senior Editor: **Helen Woodhall**
Editorial Assistant: **Georgina Burns**
Designer: **Kevin Knight**
Production: **Lorraine Baird and Sha Huxtable**

Moira and Nicholas Hankinson are hereby identified as the authors of
this work in accordance with Section 77 of the Copyright, Designs and
Patents Act 1988.

A Cataloguing In Publication record for this title is available from the
British Library.

Colour separations by Colourscan, Singapore
Printed and bound in Spain by Artes Gráficas Toledo S.A.U.
D.L. TO: 1282-2000

Picture acknowledgments:
8 *centre right* Bob Whitfield; **12** *centre right* Bob Whitfield; **36** Paul
Anderson; **37** *right* Bob Whitfield; **98** *top left* Madeleine Boulesteix; **98**
right Madeleine Boulesteix; **124** *left* Moira and Nicholas Hankinson; **139**
bottom Bob Whitfield.

Contents

The decorative detail over this entrance hall arch is not carved wood, as might be expected, but an unusual hammered leather moulding.

INTRODUCTION

Salvage has become newsworthy, and goes much further than the recycling of buildings such as the Tate Modern. For many people a sense of nostalgia is evoked at the sight of serried ranks of roll-top baths, cast-iron columns, weathered white marble chimneypiece jambs, pile upon pile of old clay bricks, tiles and crates of stone, all with a history, a story to tell.

Sadly, this was not always the case. Only as recently as thirty or forty years ago, many such items were destroyed by being put on the bonfire or simply thrown out. Much was gladly given away to gypsies, scrap metal dealers or the rag-and-bone man, who made a living from collecting cast-offs, and selling them on for recycling. If they had no second-hand value, huge quantities of 'waste' material were quite simply sent to landfill.

NEAR RIGHT

Open the skilfully painted double doors of this floor-to-ceiling cupboard bought at a flea market and you will find an array of compartments comprising shelves, drawers, hooks, as well as a fold-down table top with a perforated zinc cupboard above, which suggests it may have been used for food storage at some stage.

CENTRE RIGHT

An imaginative use of reclaimed materials can be seen in Hank and Sophia Terry's exciting bathroom. Elegant Georgian stone columns flank an enormous stone bath, once housed in an asylum, and lead scraps were cast in sea shells to make the tap heads, while the spout was made from an old copper downpipe. More copper piping was used to make the light above the cabinet, and the cabinet itself was constructed from old lead flashings. The slate shelf, skirtings and floor edging are all copings from a former school.

FAR RIGHT

A reclaimed terrazzo floor perfectly complements an informal dining room.

Then along came a new breed of dealers who were able to see that by salvaging this detritus there were the possibilities of handsome profits to be made as well as preserving our national heritage. Architectural antiques and building materials that could be reused began to find a market among designers, architects and a few enthusiasts who frequented the newly established reclamation yards and architectural salvage sales.

Further changes came about during the first of the housing booms, when the general public developed an appetite, fuelled by the proliferation of new magazines and media interest for the renovation or alteration of neglected properties. Builders' skips were raided and people stopped throwing out what had previously been considered junk. They began to realise the value of their properties, especially if they retained authentic period elements, the grander the better, reflecting wealth and status just as they always have throughout history. It was then that the demand for architectural salvage began to

grow rapidly, to such an extent that there were simply not the supplies to satisfy the market, and so specialist companies started making reproductions of architectural and period decorations.

For enthusiasts of salvage, decisions have to be made about their purchases. What should be done with the over-sized oak beam that looked so perfect back in the demolition yard? Should it be incorporated structurally or cosmetically? Should it be used at all? It is all too easy to acquire something that then lies waiting for a home for years to come, making it more of a conundrum than a bargain.

We do not argue that because something is old it therefore merits preservation, regardless of whether it is beautiful, well designed or even simply well made, but we do urge you to take a new look at everyday objects and question whether they have, in fact, reached the end of their useful life.

One of the aims of this book is to offer inspiration, and perhaps even some answers, as well as to pass on our enormous

enthusiasm, indeed passion, for the subject of salvage. It is important ecologically to reuse materials, and we hope to stimulate thoughts and ideas of your own. This book should enlighten you on how you may create something new from something old, based on an awareness of what is available to you, cost effectively, and using tools you already own or that are easily obtainable. There are both traditional and contemporary interior photographs accompanying over thirty different projects grouped together in themed chapters: Wining and Dining, Bedrooms, Bathrooms and Boudoirs, Rooms for Living, Decorative Accessories, Light and Shade, and Design and Detail. The projects and practical ideas are suitable for all levels of ability, whether you are a keen beginner or dedicated to handicraft.

So forget the pretentious, contrived, sterile perfection seen in so many 'designer' houses, where money can purchase everything, down to the very last little detail. Free your mind from modern design ideals and lose yourself in your

imagination; do not be afraid to use your creativity and accept that you will make a few mistakes along the way.

Join us in our commitment to salvage and discover the pleasure in taking an object that has already had one life and turning it into something new, beautiful and original. Through *Salvage Style in Your Home* we try to communicate our ideas and explore the almost limitless possibilities for creatively reusing, reinventing, revitalising and reinterpreting good-quality materials.

RIGHT

Everything in the bathroom of this converted mid-nineteenth century church built by a pupil of Pugin has been salvaged. Curved panelling taken from the canopy above the organ has been cleverly used to disguise pipes, and the cistern has been hidden behind a pew and finished off with a slate shelf above.

A large table automatically becomes the focal point in a dining area, because it is the place not only for eating and drinking but somewhere where family and friends spend time top is wooden, the beauty of the grain and the warmth of the wood can be seen to full advantage, contrasting with the surroundings of many of today's minimal, cool interiors. It may be

WINING AND DINING

together, gathering for discussions, celebrations and even business meetings. When sitting at a table you immediately see and have contact with a mass of surface, whether it is wood (the material traditionally used in the construction of tables) or zinc, stainless steel, stone or slate, all of which are good materials for rejuvenating an old table, depending on the surrounding decor. If the table a simple, functional design, with a scrubbed plank top, an oak, ash or elm surface supported on a trestle base, or something on a larger scale, altogether grander, perhaps made from hardwood with a highly polished surface and elegantly tapered legs. Whatever the style, a table may appear easy to design and make, but getting the design and proportions absolutely right can be quite a challenge.

NEAR RIGHT

Pine dressers rarely have such impact. The top half of this one, showing white china that is in use on a daily basis, was made up using reclaimed wood and then painted to match the old original base.

CENTRE LEFT

This circular kitchen table top was salvaged, repainted and screwed to a cast-iron base made from an agricultural root chopper (still bearing the maker's name) to make a highly individual and practical piece of furniture.

CENTRE RIGHT

Slate slabs from a Cornish farmhouse floor were made into tables and the wheels from a disused British Rail trolley used to make the feet bases; the decorative bracket was once a pub sign, and the window glass, coping stones and wooden floor are all reclaimed.

FAR RIGHT

An ornate gilded theatre box was located, refurbished and installed to great dramatic effect above the double folding doors leading from the dining room of the Charlton House Hotel.

LEFT

Despite its contemporary look, much of this kitchen by Milo Design has been reclaimed. Both the zinc sheets on the walls and the taps above the counter came from an old hospital, whilst the column and twin radiators were bought from a reclamation yard. The door handles just seen in the background are old trap door ring pulls, and the curvaceous kitchen counter came from a public house bar.

Wooden table tops need protection from very hot dishes, which can damage the surface. Practical, good-looking table mats are often difficult to find, but slate roofing tiles are easily available either directly from someone who may be reroofing or from the abundance of salvage yards to be found across the country. Cut down to size, varnished and backed with felt, they make stunning, indispensable place mats. (Mixing wedges of offcut tongue and groove timber in different colours, then joining them together, can make another unusual place mat.) To finish dressing the table, we have used ex-army aluminium dishes, which have been given an authentic pewter look and put to great effect as chargers, toning beautifully with the slate mats. Use clean empty baked bean tins filled with flowers and foliage and give new life to old bed springs as quirky candle holders (see page 122). Finally, to complete the look, recycle curtains, cushion covers, sheeting or any other suitable material from jumble sales and charity shops to make into napkins.

Traditionally dining chairs were made in oak, elm, ash, fruit-wood or a combination of two and sometimes three timbers, in hundreds of different designs, many of which are still reproduced today, though mostly in beech or pine.

Robust benches often make a convenient alternative to chairs when space is limited in an informal dining area, and they can be made quite easily using disused scaffold board. We show how a simple three-legged stool can be put together using a wooden chopping board for the seat and ash axe handles for the legs, just as salvaged tractor seats have also been made into comfortable kitchen stools.

With the warmth of the fire and the glow of the lights, wining and dining must surely be one of life's great pleasures.

SLATE TABLE MATS

EQUIPMENT

Tape measure
Straight edge
Marking point or sharp nail
Slate ripper
Pliers
Electric sander (optional)
Medium-grade glass- or emery paper
12 mm (½ in) paintbrush
Scissors
Glue brush

MATERIALS

Eight roof slates, overall size approx.
 40 x 30 cm (16 x 12 in)
Four larger roof slates, overall size approx.
 50 x 35 cm (20 x 14 in)
Satin finish or floor-grade varnish
Approx. 2 sq. m (2½ sq. yd) baize or felt
Rubberised glue

The materials above are sufficient to make a set of eight table mats and four centre mats. Adjust measurements as necessary according to the size of roof slates available. Also bear in mind the size of the table on which they will be placed.

METHOD

1 Select your slates carefully, rejecting any that are splitting, are too irregular in shape or have enlarged nail holes. Measure the slates from a good end and score a line across each width with the marking point or sharp nail. Use the slate ripper to cut slates to size, being careful to keep the cut edge as straight as possible. We suggest that the 40 x 30 cm (16 x 12 in) slates are cut down to 30 x 20 cm (12 x 8 in) and the 50 x 35 cm (20 x 14 in) slates are cut down to 35 x 25 cm (14 x 11 in).

2 All hand-split and cut slates have one face that is usually flat whilst the other has a chipped bevelled edge. The face with the bevelled edge will be the top of your place mat. Use pliers to trim the cut edge and the original edges to remove any loose material, matching the original bevelled edges if possible. Remove any loose material from both faces and finish with glass- or emery paper, either by hand or using a sander, taking care not to score the top surface too heavily. Wash each slate carefully in running water and leave to dry.

3 When both surfaces are dry, paint with two coats of satin finish or floor-grade varnish, covering any indentations and the bevelled edges. Leave to dry.

4 Cut twelve pieces of baize or felt 12 mm (½ in) smaller all round than the size of the slates. Brush rubberised glue on to the underside of the slates and fit the baize or felt on to the bottom surface; this will prevent your table mats scratching the table surface.

Safety note

We advise that you wear safety glasses or goggles when using any mechanical sanding equipment. Rubber or protective gloves are also recommended for this project.

Food is one of our growing passions – if the number of cookery books and television programmes is anything to go by – and the social importance of family meals is widely recognised, yet how much thought do we give to the presentation of the daily eating ritual? Making the table look as exciting as the dishes themselves takes just a little thought and effort, and here we suggest one idea to rejuvenate roof slates to make easy but chic replacements for melamine mats bearing images of Big Ben and the leaning tower of Pisa. These slate mats will give your table a new, crisp image, and by scouring skips parked outside properties in the process of being reroofed, demolished or restored, you are sure to find enough slates to make up a table setting for ten or more.

If raiding skips is not your style, another source of old roofing slate is your nearest reclamation yard. The slate will have suffered from exposure to wind, rain, snow and pollution, but it is still desirable. Newly cut slate can be purchased from any flooring contractor, tile shop or builders' merchant, where you will be faced with a mind-boggling choice of colour, size and thickness.

Damaged or chipped roofing slates can be cut down to the required size and the underside covered in felt or baize to protect the table surface. Once cleaned and polished, the slate's inherent insulating qualities, combined with its practical wipe-clean surface, make it a smart table accessory to be admired (and no doubt copied) when you next decide to hold a dinner party.

INFORMAL DINING

There is a proliferation of companies providing conservatories whose selling pitch has long been to persuade us to take the 'inside out', but the owners of this country kitchen decided to bring the 'outside in' when it came to decorating an informal family eating area.

Inspired by the potting shed and a collection of old tools – most of which were handmade, although some of their origins were rather obscure – their interpretation of the look began to take shape with the tool display, not the table, being the main focal point. Although the building was fairly old, its interior had been insensitively modernised at some stage in its history, leaving little of its original charm. With a blank canvas and a limited budget, they set to work.

Natural light was poor, so the walls were painted off-white and an old ledge-and-brace exterior door, complete with its original chipped and flaking paint, was installed. In order to make the 'shed' more intimate, they disguised the ceiling with suspended rows of redundant wooden ladders; this gave the room a warmer, more welcoming feel and provided somewhere to hang baskets,

herbs and other decorative items. The ladders were obtained very inexpensively from a quaintly old-fashioned horticultural nursery that had ceased trading after the death of the elderly owner, for they were regarded as unsafe once they were superseded by modern metal versions.

The classic refectory table was made from disused scaffold boards and the chapel chairs have an ecclesiastical past, as the name suggests. A stool and a chopping block were made using axe handles in ash for the legs; soft, atmospheric lighting in the form of a floor-standing candle lamp was created from a one-time flower display stand, and a stencil candle light made an interesting table centrepiece. To complete the look, assorted garden sieves and an ancient saw were used as attractive wall displays and faux pewter plates adorned the window sill.

TOOL DISPLAY

EQUIPMENT

25 mm (1 in) paintbrush
Waxing brush or stiff-bristled paintbrush
Soft cotton rag
Fine-grade wire wool
Proprietary metal polish
Wire brush
Electric drill
Circular wire brush or sanding flap
    drill head
3 mm (⅛ in) wood drill bit
Screwdriver
Pliers

MATERIALS

Selection of old tools
Wooden braced plank display board
Colourless timber preservative
Antique brown furniture wax
Clear wax or metal lacquer spray
Selection of screws and rawlplugs
Medium metal wire or gardening wire
Length of batten approx. 25 mm (1 in) x
    75 mm (3 in) x the width of the display
    board

Safety note

We advise that you wear safety glasses or goggles
when using any mechanical sanding equipment.
Rubber or other protective gloves are
recommended for this project.

Old farm equipment, kitchen utensils and garden tools are still easy to find, inexpensive to buy and have a character sadly missing in much of the equipment produced today.

Enthusiastic readers of the local press will find farm and market garden sales advertised. As small growers and farmers retire, their families may be reluctant to continue to work on what are often uncommercial holdings and the land is sold to surrounding farmers or purchased by urban dwellers seeking a rural retreat. A result of this change is the disposal of what were often the everyday tools used by past generations. Many of the tools were made by local foundries or fabricated by the landowner using skills now forgotten and the purpose of some of them is quite obscure. Walls displaying old shovels, pitchforks, rakes of odd shapes and sizes, some complete, a few broken and many of a particularly local design, are a constant source of intrigue.

For this project we have used a selection of farm and garden tools displayed on an old wooden surface. The tools include a redundant spring grain weight with a brass face which was only revealed after the offending dirt was laboriously removed, a hand-forged drainage spade, a pruning saw, a short flat-tined fork, the origin of which remains unknown, a brass and iron stirrup pump, a primitive sickle and a pair of fencing pliers. These tools were only a small part of a selection of begrimed and broken tools bought as one lot at a farm auction for less than half the price of a modern hand trowel.

TOOL DISPLAY

METHOD

1 Treat the display board with colourless timber preservative and leave to dry. Then apply antique brown furniture wax with the waxing brush or stiff-bristled paintbrush, rubbing it well into the wood with a soft cotton rag and polish to a soft sheen with more soft cotton rag. A second coat of wax can be applied, which will give a deeper colour and longer-lasting finish. Put to one side.

2 To clean brass or copper surfaces, use a proprietary metal polish and fine-grade wire wool, finishing with more polish applied with a soft cloth. Seal polished surfaces with metal lacquer to prevent subsequent tarnishing. Wooden handles and parts should be washed in warm soapy water then waxed and polished with furniture wax. Clean iron or steel tools with a wire brush to remove loose rust and dirt, then finish with an electric drill fitted with a circular wire brush or sanding flap drill head.

3 Use the drill and wire or sanding flap head to remove corrosion until the desired finish is achieved. The metal surface of the tool will be pitted more or less deeply depending on the amount of corrosion it has suffered; the aim of this cleaning is not to return the tool to its original condition but to remove surface rust and reveal the colour of the base metal. To preserve the finish and prevent subsequent corrosion, either apply clear wax to the surface or spray with metal lacquer.

4 Place the board on two blocks above a flat surface, so that you can work on both sides, and experiment with arranging the cleaned tools on the front until you have a display that pleases you. Wooden-handled tools can be fixed to the board using screws driven in from the reverse. Remove each tool, carefully noting its position, and use the electric drill and 3 mm (⅛ in) drill bit to drill a hole from the top where the handle will be placed. Replace the tool and, working from the back of the board, drive a screw through the board and into the handle, securing the tool to the board.

5 Metal tools can be fitted to the board using medium wire or garden wire. Use a malleable coated wire of a muted colour or one with a dull finish, otherwise the wire will be obvious and spoil the appearance of the finished display. Select a part of the tool that will support it when the board is returned to the vertical and drill holes close to each side of the tool. Cut a length of wire, bend it into a 'U' shape, then pass it over the tool and through both holes so that each end emerges by at least 50 mm (2 in) on the reverse. Use pliers to twist the ends of wire together to secure the tool to the board.

When all the tools are fitted, remove the board from the blocks and place it upright to ensure that all the tools are securely in place. Tighten any screws or wire, as necessary, or add more fixings if required. Take the length of batten and fix it to the wall in the desired position with screws and rawlplugs. Place the board on the wall, resting a brace on the fixed batten. Once you are satisfied with its position, secure it with two screws through the board into the batten.

FLOWER DISPLAY CANDLE STAND

EQUIPMENT

Wire brush
Small stiff brush (an old toothbrush
   is ideal)
12 mm (½ in) paintbrush
Soft brush or cotton rag

MATERIALS

Flower stand
Stove blacking paste
Selection of small metal tart and
   confectionery cups
Matt black paint or spray paint
White spirit
Night lights or tea lights
Candle
Scented oils

Safety note

Rubber or protective gloves are
recommended for this project.

Auctions are a good hunting ground for interesting items. We bought several 'bargains' at the auction of the contents of a nursery and garden centre, including a number of cast-iron stands once used to display bunches of fresh cut flowers.

The stands had not been used for many years and the original paintwork had almost completely rusted away. Constructed of a hollow iron column set in a heavy cast hexagonal base, each stand came with a number of bent metal display platforms designed to fit over the column and fit at any height with a turn screw. Perhaps not surprisingly, there was little demand at the auction for such idiosyncratic items and we were able to buy them for next to nothing. It is unlikely that similar stands are easy to find, but the new use we found for them illustrates how, by using a little imagination, the most unwanted items can be salvaged and resuscitated. Place plain or fluted individual metal confectionery tins from government surplus stores (individual aluminium apple tart bases will do just as well) into the metal platforms and fill some with night lights and others with aromatic essential oils – an idea to please the eye and soothe the senses. Alternatively, remove the platforms, keeping just the heavy bases and pole and have an electrician wire the stand (unless you are confident enough to undertake this yourself) and convert it into a low standard lamp. Painted and fitted with a simple shade, it takes on a cool contemporary look, far removed from its original purpose.

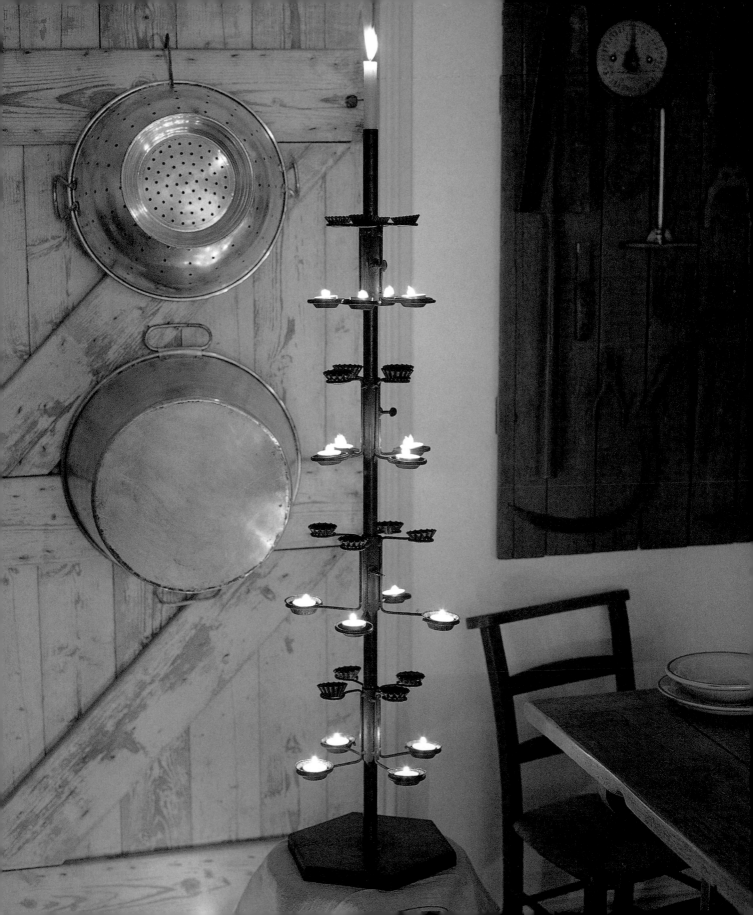

FLOWER DISPLAY CANDLE STAND

METHOD

1 We chose to convert this stand into a candelabra and give it a muted satin black finish. Had the stand been completely rusted rather than patchy with some of the original paint still adhering to it, we would have wire brushed it and sealed the finish with a metal lacquer to preserve its rusted appearance. Remove the metal platforms (each comprising two sets of four branches welded to a central pipe) from the column, and ensure the turn screws work freely; apply releasing oil if necessary. Use the wire brush to remove loose rust and peeling paint from the base, column and platforms, making sure to wire brush any residual paint to provide a key for the stove blacking finish.

2 Place the stand and platforms on newspaper or other protective surface and, with the small stiff brush, apply the stove blacking to all exposed parts, paying particular attention to the corroded metal to ensure total coverage of all surfaces. Leave to dry to a matt black finish. When the blacking is completely dry, polish the stand and platforms to a soft sheen with a soft brush or rag. Continue until little or no polish is deposited on the rag and the blacking does not come off when the stand is handled. Replace the platforms on the stand in the positions desired, and secure with the turn screws.

3 For candle holders we used a selection of round and fluted metal tart and confectionery cups, old and rusty and long past their useful life, which we found in a government surplus store and which fitted the platform rings perfectly. (Only later did we discover that aluminium tart cups used by most manufacturing bakeries would have been just as suitable.) Brush or spray paint the cups matt black, both inside and out, and leave to dry. Place a night light or tea light into each cup and fit the cups into the rings. We fitted night lights into the larger cups and filled the smaller fluted cups with scented oils. Finally, fit a candle into the top of the stand column and light the night lights; as the oils in the fluted cups warm, their perfume will permeate the room.

STENCIL LIGHT

EQUIPMENT

Scissors or craft knife

MATERIALS

Eighteen equally sized stencils, either
    letters or numbers
Adhesive metal tape
Candle and candle holder

METHOD

1 Select half the stencils and place them front side down on a flat surface. Carefully arrange them together to make a rectangle three stencils wide by three stencils deep. Most old stencils were hand cut and so sizes are slightly irregular; when fitting them together make sure that the edges of your rectangle are square.

2 Use the scissors or craft knife to cut lengths of adhesive metal tape to the height and width of the rectangle. Carefully remove the backing and lay the tape along the joints between the stencils to join them together, using a finger to rub down the tape to ensure good adhesion. Repeat with the remaining nine stencils to make a second, similarly sized rectangle.

3 Cut two lengths of tape to the height of the rectangles. Remove the backing from one and join the two rectangles to make one piece six stencils wide by three deep. Carefully bring the two ends of the rectangle together to make a cylinder; place your hand inside and join the ends together with the remaining cut length of tape. Again, rub down all newly taped joints with your finger to ensure adequate adhesion.

Stand the candle holder and candle on a flat surface and place the newly constructed stencil light over them. The metal tape should be sufficiently malleable to allow the stencils to be manipulated into a regular hexagonal shape. Light the candle and enjoy the muted illumination cast from this simple, yet charming, candle light.

Stencils have been in use for many years to mark cartons, boxes, crates, bales and all sorts of shipped and carried goods. Made from a variety of materials including zinc, steel, tin, cardboard and even brass, stencils are still in use today, even in this age of technology, although most modern designs are manufactured from moulded plastic and lack the allure of their earlier counterparts. We have managed to amass several full sets of stencils over the years; most are made of zinc but one particularly valued set is made from copper sheet. For this project we have used a set of more commonly available zinc stencils that came from a farm sale and were bought in their original box complete with brushes and inks. The stencils had been heavily used and were stained with ink, but we chose to use them in this condition rather than attempt to clean them.

The particular joy of stencils when used for a lighting project such as this is that the lettering cut-outs cast curious illuminations and make a charming display of light and shade. This project demonstrates the making of a very basic candle light, but the more ambitious craftsperson might attempt the construction of a light column, shade or wall light.

PEWTER PLATES

EQUIPMENT

Metal cleaning paste
Medium-grade wire wool
Soft cotton rag

MATERIALS

Aluminium plates or bowls
Metal polish
Antique brown furniture wax
Metal lacquer spray

METHOD

1 Carefully select the plates you will be using for this project. All will show the effects of years of wear and tear and will be scored with cutlery marks very similar to the surface markings seen on most antique pewter, but this is part of its charm. Many plates are stamped with a government or maker's mark on their top surface; these should be rejected. Instead choose plates that are unmarked and are not too damaged or dented.

2 Place a small amount of metal cleaner (we used a proprietary stainless steel cleaner) on an old plate or other container, dip a wad of wire wool in the cleaner and begin to work on the surface of the plate. Always rub round the surface and keep the wad of wire wool saturated with cleaner. Continue working until any surface oxidation is removed and the wire wool is working into the surface of the aluminium. Periodically wipe the surface clean with the soft cotton rag to examine the finish. Be careful not to rub out all the surface scratches and markings.

3 When you are satisfied with the appearance you have achieved, wipe the plate clean and apply polish with the soft cloth, rubbing it well into the surface. Wipe the surface clean and

polish with more clean soft cloth. Now you must examine the plate and decide on its final colour and finish. The cleaner and polish will have darkened the appearance of the plate, but an even darker finish can be achieved by rubbing a little antique brown furniture wax into the surface. Apply the wax liberally and wipe off, leaving a residue on the surface before allowing it to dry and polishing it. You may wish to stop at this point because the wax will prevent further tarnishing.

4 Should you wish to achieve a gloss finish, spray the plate with metal lacquer and leave it to dry. Your faux pewter plates will deceive all but the most knowledgeable observer, unless they pick them up in which case their lightness will reveal the fraud. Display the plates on a dresser or shelf, use plate stretchers to hang them on a wall or use them as chargers under plates at the dining table. Lacquered plates may be washed in hot water, and waxed plates should be dusted clean, but remember that they should not be used for eating purposes.

Safety note

We advise that rubber or protective gloves are used for this project and that you work on newspaper or some other disposable surface.

Pewter is an alloy of tin and lead, sometimes with the addition of a little copper or antimony, which in past years was used for plates, mugs and other vessels as a substitute for the wooden or porous earthenware vessels used previously. Lead is highly toxic, so it would be unwise to use early pewter for food or drink. Because of the awareness of this danger, modern pewter uses considerably less lead in its manufacture.

Early pewter is very collectable and fetches high prices at auctions or in antique shops. When polished, it assumes a dull, attractive sheen, and a collection of old pewter arranged on a dresser or mantle makes a memorable display.

Quite recently we discovered a number of discarded aluminium plates and bowls that we thought might lend themselves to conversion into faux pewter, and this project demonstrates our method. We later learnt that these plates were examples of thousands that were once produced for the army during and just after the 1940s and which occasionally turn up in government surplus stores all over the country.

AXE-HANDLE STOOL

EQUIPMENT

Tape measure
Electric drill
25 mm (1 in) spade wood bit
12 mm (½ in) straight or rounded wood
    chisel
Hammer or mallet
Variable-speed multi-purpose electric tool
    with 18 mm (¾ in) sanding head (or
    round wood file)
Soft cotton rag
Medium-grade glass paper

MATERIALS

Timber round approx. 35 cm (14 in)
    diameter x 38 mm (1½ in) deep
Three axe handles or three 60 cm (24 in)
    lengths of broom handle
Scrap timber
Wood glue

Many of the 'bargains' found in a reclamation yard or scavenged from a skip or rubbish tip remain in our workshop to this day, half forgotten, awaiting the visionary ideas for which they were originally so enthusiastically acquired.

One such purchase was a stack of dirt-encrusted axe handles found at a government surplus yard buried under a pile of discarded ammunition boxes and offered for sale as firewood. Their interesting shapes caught our eye and on closer inspection we realised they were made of solid ash. Determined they would not end up as fuel for the fire, we managed to secure some and now we wish we had bought more.

The shape of the axe handles seemed to suggest legs and so we used three for the legs of a kitchen chopping block. In this project we show how they can be used to construct a charming if unconventional stool. A discarded beech round, probably originally made as a chopping board, was used to make the seat. The axe handles will also make the sides of a log basket, and should you manage to buy a quantity, they would make an eye-catching balustrade. If you have difficulty in finding axe handles, the stool can be made just as easily from broom handles, offcut timber or even straight branches pruned from a tree.

When making this stool, the legs should be slightly splayed for stability, and all the holes for housing the legs should be cut at a slight angle to allow for this splay. For the seat of the stool, a similar round can be cut from a solid or laminated timber offcut.

AXE-HANDLE STOOL

METHOD

1 Mark three points on the top surface at an equal distance round the circumference of the timber round and approximately 25 mm (1 in) from the edge. Place the handles or other material being used for the legs inside these marked points and draw round them with a pencil to mark where the legs will be inserted.

2 Place the round on a piece of scrap timber and use the spade bit, driven in at a slight angle, to make an initial hole. To prevent the timber splitting, drill through from one face of the timber until the point of the spade bit just emerges and then complete the hole drilling from the opposite side. Repeat, drilling holes for all three legs. If you are using broom handles for the legs, use a spade bit the size of the handles.

3 Use the variable-speed multi-purpose electric sander or chisel and wood file to enlarge the hole to the size of the pencil mark, making sure that the angle of splay is maintained. If you are making the legs from broom handle, there should be no necessity to enlarge the spade-drilled holes.

4 Apply wood glue liberally to the first 25 mm (1 in) of one of the axe handles and insert it into the round from the underside. Tap it gently home with a hammer or mallet until the top is flush with, or proud of, the upper surface of the round. Axe handles are made with a slit cut in their top to allow a wedge to be inserted when fitted to the axe head. Cut a small wedge from offcut timber to the width of this slit, apply glue and drive it into the top of the handle to secure it firmly into the round. If you are using broom handle, cut a 38 mm (1½ in) slit in its top to allow wedging into the round for added security and strength.

Wipe off any excess glue and leave the stool on one side for the glue to dry. Sand off any excess glue or timber proud of the top surface and finish as desired. The completed stool can be waxed, stained or painted. If you choose staining, ensure that any glue on the wood surface is removed before you apply the stain, because the dried glue will not absorb the stain and so the finish will be patchy. The stool top we made for this project was completed with a distressed paint finish and the legs were waxed with antique brown furniture wax.

Whether the style is comfortably traditional or has a Zen-like simplicity, bedrooms are where we spend a third of our lives. Careful thought and

The amount of light largely depends on the direction in which the bedroom faces, and light, whether daylight or interior lighting, will to some extent dictate its mood and colours.

BEDROOMS, BATHROOMS AND BOUDOIRS

consideration need to be given to how we treat our bedrooms, which are certainly the most personal rooms in the house, if not the most important. Besides the bed, a bedroom may have space for additional furniture, perhaps an armchair, sofa or table, as well as storage items such as chests of drawers and wardrobes, making them not just rooms to sleep in but also a place to read and relax.

Furnishing fabrics are fun to think about: bedcovers, cushions, loose covers and throws for the chairs. Linen has for years been a firm favourite, especially old French country linen sheets of superb quality, roughly textured, often with a red embroidered monogram at one end and occasionally a fringe. They make simple but effective beautifully draping curtains, allowing light to filter through.

Children have their own ideas when it comes to decorating their bedrooms, and it is strong, bright colours that usually appeal to them. They like their own special piece of furniture, such as an old school desk that has been rescued and transformed from a grubby object emblazoned with graffiti into something revitalised, practical and fun. Older children and teenagers want to use their bedrooms as somewhere to escape from the grown-ups; here, surrounded by chaotic mess, they can play loud music, hence the need for CD storage. We show you how to make practical CD storage out of a dilapidated old wooden French shutter (see pages 54–57).

The bed is an obvious feature or focal point in the bedroom. Beds are made from many different materials, most commonly wood, but also iron and brass, and a bed made from an unusual material such as aluminium will give a very contemporary feel to a bedroom. Beds come in all shapes and sizes and although there are specialist companies who will make up unusual mattress dimensions, including round or even boat-shaped ones, it is useful to bear in mind if constructing a bed to your own design from salvaged materials that mattresses are easier and cheaper to obtain in standard sizes. Whatever its size and shape, it is important to always buy the best-quality mattress you can afford.

Finding timber suitable for constructing beds is often easier than you might think. Old railway sleepers and ceiling beams of oak and elm can all be cut to size and used to make the framework, just as redundant carved doors, church pews, decorative wooden panels and even disused five-bar farm gates are the perfect raw materials for making into practical and interesting beds or headboards. A highly unusual fold-away guest bed is shown opposite, imaginatively made from an exquisitely painted panel depicting animals from Noah's Ark which was salvaged from a fairground ride.

The idea that bathrooms should be spartan, purely functional, hygienic rooms containing a cast-iron bath, pedestal wash basin, lavatory and lino-covered floor is fortunately long gone.

Bathrooms today are expected to be every bit as comfortable as any other room in the house. Just take the briefest look through any of the glossy magazines and you will see rooms purporting to be bathrooms but looking more like stage sets – all opulence and atmosphere – or cosy and homely, the epitome of rustic country charm. Idiosyncratic items add interest and character, such as a single trestle bracketed to the wall and used as a rail to show off pretty towels and linens (see pages 42–43). Enormous cupboards in rich mahogany or other hardwoods, too big and cumbersome for the average-sized room today, can be cut down in size to panel a bath, perhaps continuing around the walls to dado height, and can even made into cupboard doors under the basins to provide additional storage.

Because we lead increasingly busy lives with more and more pressures, there seems to be a need to simplify things, to have order, comfort and harmony in our homes. One way of achieving this is to optimise space and create storage – a place for everything and everything in its place. Old hardwood 'first class' railway compartments can be salvaged and made into capacious cupboards for the dressing room or boudoir. Enormous, superbly carved mahogany wardrobes, which would cost the earth if the equivalent quality were made today, look just as handsome and majestic when made to fit an alcove or any other space.

TOP LEFT

This unusual spare bed, which folds up against the wall when not in use, is an original 1933 fairground Noah's Ark design, comprising two horses and chariots. On the bed is a salvaged traditional southern Italian family-sized bedcover, and in the background is a mural painted by Corrina Sargood to disguise a wall-to-wall cupboard containing an office desk and storage.

TOP RIGHT

Black and white are used with striking effect in Elizabeth and Crispin Deacon's guest bathroom, its 1930s sanitary fittings juxtaposed with contemporary lighting.

RIGHT

A view of the bathroom of Hank and Sophia Terry, the owners of Milo Design. The shower walls and mirror frame are made from old lead roofing sheet and the soap dish/shampoo rack has been created from a lightning conductor salvaged from a church. The wash basin was cleverly fashioned from the base of an old copper hot water tank and the tap heads were cast from lead roof flashing in a child's jelly mould.

RAILWAY BED

EQUIPMENT

Tape measure
Set square
Hammer
32 mm (1¼ in) wood chisel
Handsaw
Glasspaper
Electric drill and bits
Screwdriver
Adjustable spanner
38 mm (1½ in) paintbrush
Soft cotton rag

MATERIALS

Four posts
Approx. 2 m (6 ft 6 in) of 22.5 cm x 25 mm
    (9 x 1 in) planed timber
Wood glue
65 mm (2½ in) wood screws
90 cm (3 ft) single metal bed frame and
    headboard fittings (chills)
Wood stain
Clear furniture wax

Amidst the pile of debris our eyes were drawn to the tapering wooden poles protruding above the rusty metal ammunition boxes, military bed bases stacked one upon the other, enough rainwater-filled latrines to equip an entire barracks and assorted shovels.

Filthy, wet and shivering, we stood in the biting wind on a November morning speculating on what the poles had been used for and how they could be used again. Inspiration struck: their slender shapes lent themselves perfectly to a design for a bed, a four-poster bed to be precise. We quickly acquired a job lot. We later learnt from Lawrence, owner of Harper's Bazaar and purveyor of all things surplus to government needs, that they were solid ash levers used on the railways to move wagons around the sidings by hand before mechanisation made them obsolete. If you cannot obtain ash levers such as these, the bed could just as easily be constructed using any pillar-like objects, such as fence posts or staircase newel posts.

The metal bed frame and headboard fittings were located in a salvage yard. Almost forty years old, they had once been turned out in their thousands. They were robustly constructed for use in army barracks but had never been used and apart from some surface rust, were in perfect condition. If you can't find a similar frame, you can buy one new from a small number of specialist contract furniture makers. This bed could also be made with a slatted timber base set into wooden side pieces fitted to the headboard using any of the numerous connectors on the market.

RAILWAY BED

METHOD

Before commencing work on this project, read through the instructions and think carefully about how you will approach the making of your bed and its dimensions. Remember that you will need to find or purchase a mattress for the bed and that most are made to standard sizes. As a guide, single beds are normally constructed so that the mattress top is approximately 45–50 cm (18–20 in) from floor level and you will have to adapt the project for the mattress you propose to use. Should you wish to provide storage under the bed, it can be made higher, although it is a good idea to keep to a height such that you can sit comfortably on the edge of the bed.

1 Make a mark with a pencil at the proposed height of the bed frame on the inside face of one of the posts. Place the headboard fitting (chill) on the post so that the bed frame, when attached, will be fixed at that height. Mark the screw holes and make two marks, one above and one below the screw holes, 10 cm (4 in) apart, centred on the screw holes. Use the set square to transfer these measurements across the inside and down two sides of the post. Measure the exact thickness of the 22.5 cm (9 in) timber plank and draw a line that measurement deep on the two sides across the 10 cm (4 in) pencil lines. Use the hammer and wood chisel to score a line along this mark which shows the areas to be cut out of the post to house the 22.5 cm (9 in) head and foot boards. Turn the post inside face up and with a handsaw make a series of cuts approximately 12 mm (½ in) apart and 25 mm (1 in) deep, using the chiselled line as a guide for the exact depth, for the full length of the 10 cm (4 in) marked area.

2 When you have made saw cuts across the whole width of the post, insert the wood chisel into the cuts and gently lever out the waste wood. Clean the cut rebate with the wood chisel and glasspaper, making sure to keep to the depth indicated by the scored lines. Now repeat this process using another post; these two will hold the headboard.

3 Measure the exact width of your bed frame from fixing bolt (or bolt hole) to fixing bolt. Measure the width of a post and add it to this measurement. Use the set square to mark that final measurement on the planed timber plank and cut it to size. Lay the cut plank on a work surface and use the set square and pencil to mark a line the width of the post across each end. Mark two lines 10 cm (4 in) apart at each end centred on the width of the plank, and extend them to join the lines marking the width of the post. Use the handsaw to cut away the two outer sections at each end, each of which will measure approximately 65 mm (2½ in) x the width of the post, to create a simple T joint at each end. Err on the side of caution when cutting: it is better to cut these pieces out too small, and to have to sand down the joints to fit the rebates cut in the posts, than to remove too much timber and be left with loose joints.

4 Put plenty of wood glue into the rebate cut in the first post, then insert one of the cut joints. Check with the set square that the joint is true, then drill and fix with 65 mm (2½ in) wood screws. It is advisable before finally joining to replace the headboard fitting (chill) and check that its screw holes do not correspond with the screws holding the joint. Repeat this process, inserting the other joint into the second post, and you have created the headboard for your bed.

Wipe off any excess wood glue and put the assembled pieces to one side for the glue to dry completely. Now follow the same directions to construct the footboard with the second two posts and remaining length of timber plank.

5 Replace the headboard fittings (chills) on the foot- and headboards and secure with screws driven through the joints into the wood of the posts.

6 You will probably need assistance with this part of the project. Lean the headboard up against a vertical surface and balance one end of the bed frame on its headboard fittings (chills). Raise the other end of the frame and manoeuvre the footboard so that the bed frame can be dropped into place over its fittings. Half tighten the integral nuts fitted into the bed frame to secure it first to the footboard then to the headboard. Use a spanner to tighten all the nuts to make a rigid frame.

When we had assembled the bed we decided that because the colours of the ash wood bed posts and the salvaged pitch pine end boards were so different, we would stain the whole bed a mid-oak colour to give some uniformity to its appearance. This had the additional advantage of masking the lighter tones of the exposed timber where ends had been sawn. After applying the stain with a cotton rag, we finished the bed with a light coat of clear furniture wax and polished it with more soft cotton rag. Installed in a spare room and fitted with a mattress, the bed was made up with a cotton-covered duvet and down-filled pillow and made welcoming with a natural sheepskin thrown over its foot.

TRESTLE TOWEL RAIL

EQUIPMENT

Tape measure
Handsaw
Paint scraper
Electric sander
Glasspaper
42 mm (1¾ in) paintbrush
Lint-free cotton rag
Electric hammer drill
Masonry drill bit
Wood drill bit to fit 65 mm (2½ in) screws
Screwdriver

MATERIALS

Wooden trestle
White translucent wood finish or white matt
  emulsion paint and satin finish acrylic
  varnish
Length 65 x 38 mm (2½ x 1½ in) planed
  softwood timber
65 mm (2½ in) rawlpugs
65 mm (2½ in) screws
Four 38 mm (1½ in) angle (or corner)
  brackets
18 mm (¾ in) screws

METHOD

1 Measure the site where the towel rail will be installed, then measure the trestle. If it is too long to fit in the selected site, allowing for at least a 15 cm (6 in) gap below the trestle and a similar or greater gap above, trim it to size with the handsaw. Remove flaked or loose paint with the paint scraper and sand to a smooth finish with the electric sander and glasspaper. It is not necessary to remove all residual paint, just to produce a smooth base for the wood finish. Use the electric sander to smooth off all newly sawn sharp edges and corners.

2 Apply a liberal coat of white translucent wood finish or matt white emulsion paint. Leave for several minutes until part dried, then wipe over the surface with the clean cotton rag to remove some of the surface colour, leaving a residual finish on the timber surface. Use your judgement to create the finish you want – the process can be repeated until the desired result is achieved. Leave the trestle to dry. If you have used matt emulsion paint, seal with two coats of satin finish acrylic varnish.

3 Measure the width of the trestle at the top and bottom rungs, then use the handsaw to cut two lengths of the 65 x 38 mm (2½ x 1½ in) planed softwood timber to these measurements to make wall battens. Ideally, these should be painted in the same colour as the wall on which the trestle towel rail is to be fitted; if not, they should be finished to match the trestle. Add 15 cm (6 in) to the height of the trestle and use the drill and masonry drill bit to attach the top batten to the wall at this point with rawlplugs and 65 mm (2½ in) screws. Offer up the trestle and mark the position of the bottom rung on the wall, then attach the bottom batten in the same way. This will raise the trestle base approximately 15 cm (6 in) off the floor. Fit the 38 mm (1½ in) angle (or corner) brackets to the rear of the trestle behind the top and bottom rungs with the 18 mm (¾ in) screws, positioning them so that when the trestle is mounted on the battens the brackets will be concealed behind the rungs. Secure the trestle to the battens with more 18 mm (¾ in) screws.

Safety note

We advise that you wear safety glasses or goggles when using any mechanical sanding equipment; a dust mask is also sensible in case the surface to be sanded has been previously finished with a lead-based paint. Rubber or protective gloves are also recommended for this project.

Flicking through the pages of the glossy magazines over recent years you will have seen a number of bamboo or wooden ladders used as props in interior photographs because they lend themselves to obvious display stands. Ours is not a ladder but a trestle, often used in the painting and decorating trade as the portable base for a plank top. It had been painted at some stage and, rather than sand the paint off, we chose to keep its worn and aged patina and seal it with a satin varnish because it toned so well with other pieces of furniture with a similar 'driftwood' effect. Trestles can be found in various sizes, and should you wish to secure yours on brackets to the wall for use as a clothes rack, towel rail or any other practical use you may think of, you will first need to consider the height of the ceiling and the proportions of the room.

A PRE-TEEN BEDROOM

Children usually have a very good idea of how they like their bedrooms to look, especially when they approach their teenage years. This bedroom is not typical – it's tidy for a start! However, it does house some noteworthy reclaimed artefacts, such as the sturdy old school desk, painted with a distress finish, a wall-hung roof slate blackboard for jotting down homework deadlines, wire letter baskets to hold exercise books and, in pride of place, a painted wooden window shutter fixed to the wall and used to store the young occupant's CD collection. Another clever storage idea is the pair of wooden ladders (originally one long one, cut in half) with zinc shelving from a government surplus store slotted over the rungs. The shelving was originally used as racking for storing tinned food in a civil defence underground shelter, built in case of a nuclear attack, but with the end of the Cold War the shelter was closed down and the contents disposed of. Extra shelves can be added as the book collection expands.

SCHOOL DESK

EQUIPMENT

Screwdriver
Sash clamps
Electric sander
Medium-grade glasspaper
38 mm (1½ in) paintbrush
Waxing brush or stiff-bristled paintbrush
Soft cotton rag

MATERIALS

Traditional wooden school desk
Wood glue
Wood filler
Dark blue (or selected colour) matt
    emulsion paint
Antique brown furniture wax
Matt black emulsion paint

Safety note

We advise that you wear safety glasses or goggles
when using any mechanical sanding equipment.
Rubber or protective gloves are also
recommended for this project.

The design for a traditional child's desk, made of beech and oak and produced in their thousands for schools up and down the country, has never been surpassed for rugged practicality. These desks are, however, slowly being replaced, as budgets allow, by tables or desks often manufactured in plywood or laminate.

These days, hard-pressed schools are constrained to keep to tight financial budgets, and many caretakers spend much of their time repairing old, graffiti-covered desks and cannibalising others to keep them in use for as long as possible. You may be fortunate to find a school that has just received a new consignment of furniture; if so, there is every chance that, in return for a small donation to school funds, they will be pleased to release from the store a battered but not irreparable sample.

A salvaged solid timber school desk is well worth the time and effort required to repair and refurbish it, because it is ideally suited to a child's bedroom, providing useful storage and an essential surface on which to write, even in this technology-driven age. We have chosen to give the desk a distressed paint finish to soften its appearance.

SCHOOL DESK

METHOD

1 The extent of the damage to the desk will dictate how much repair should be undertaken, but, whatever its apparent condition, we suggest that all metalwork should be removed and the desk taken apart.

2 Inspect all joints for damage and repair as necessary. Carefully apply wood glue to all joints and reassemble using sash clamps to secure the joints. Use the electric sander and medium-grade glasspaper to remove all the varnish and most of the inevitable graffiti, carved initials and other evidence of children's use. Fill any large holes or scratches with wood filler.

3 Paint the exterior of the desk with one coat of dark blue (or selected colour) matt emulsion. Leave to dry for at least twenty-four hours.

4 When the paint is fully dry, use glasspaper to remove paint carefully from edges, where wear would naturally occur. For authenticity, pay particular attention to corners, stretchers (if your desk has any) and legs, where feet would normally cause wear.

5 Use the waxing brush or stiff-bristled paintbrush to apply a liberal application of antique brown furniture wax to a small area, then rub it into the paint with a soft cotton rag. It is best to work with a well-waxed rag to prevent dragging. The wax will react with the surface of the paint to give a distressed appearance; the previously sanded areas will pick up some colour from the paint, but this will serve to give a look of natural wear. Leave to dry and continue working on other areas until the desk is finished. When all the wax is dry, polish with the stiff brush and finish with a clean soft cotton rag.

Paint the inside of the desk with matt black emulsion paint. It will prove almost impossible to remove all the ink stains and other marks on the inside surface, so painting it black or another dark colour is the best course of action.

Reassemble the desk, replacing all the metal parts using the original or similar cross-head screws. The finished desk may be cleaned with a moistened soft cloth and will benefit from an occasional application of clear furniture wax to maintain its appearance.

SLATE BOARD

EQUIPMENT

Paint scraper
Coarse metal file
Coarse-grade glasspaper
Medium- and fine-grade emery paper
38 mm (1½ in) paintbrush (optional)
Electric hammer drill
Masonry drill bit
Screwdriver

MATERIALS

Old slate
Satin interior varnish or milk (optional)
Rawlplugs
Two 50 mm (2 in) screws
Two washers to fit screws (optional)
Chalk or slate pencil

METHOD

1 Select an old slate in relatively good condition with regular edges and nail holes that are not too enlarged. Place the slate on a protected work area and prise off any loose delaminated slate or flaking with a paint scraper. Gently tap the surface of the slate with your knuckle; if you hear a hollow sound, more surface slate will have to be removed. Continue until you reveal a solid surface. Use the coarse metal file to clean the edges of the slate and remove any irregularities, always filing towards the edge of the slate.

2 When you have cleaned the slate as best you can with the paint scraper and coarse file, place it on your work area with the bevel-edged side up and use coarse glasspaper to smooth the surface to a rough finish. Complete the process with wetted medium-grade, followed by fine-grade, emery paper.

Wash the slate down with clean water and allow it to dry. If desired, the slate can be painted with one coat of satin interior varnish. Alternatively, follow the old Welsh tradition and apply a thin coat of milk to one surface. When dry, the milk seals the slate and provides an excellent, slightly shiny finish.

3 To fix the slate board to a wall, hold it against the wall in the desired position and mark the screw holes. Drill into the wall with the drill and masonry bit, insert rawlplugs and fit the slate board to the wall with screws driven through the nail holes into the rawlplugged holes. If the nail holes are a little large, place a washer behind the head of each screw before securing the slate to the wall. Write messages, or draw fanciful pictures, whatever your whim, on the fitted slate board with chalk or a slate pencil. A useful hint when using chalk is to wet it before use: when dry, the image or writing will stand out much better.

Safety note

Rubber or protective gloves are
recommended for this project.

Before the days of inexpensively mass-produced paper, schoolchildren wrote their daily lessons on slate boards. Slate was readily available and economical, and had the added advantage that, after use, it could be wiped clean and used again. In some less wealthy countries slate boards are still in use in impoverished schools.

Slate is mined in many parts of the world and ranges in colour from almost black, through green and blue to palest grey. The slate we have used for this stylish wall-mounted board is from Wales, mined more than fifty years ago and removed from the roof of a house undergoing restoration. Almost all roofing slates are hand split and shaped to size; the nail holes are generally made at the time the slate is fitted to a roof, but all slates, whether old or new, show evidence on their face of the splitter's blow. All hand-split slates have one flat face and one with a bevelled edge.

We have used the existing nail holes in this slate to fit it to the wall. With a little effort, any slate can be easily transformed into a slick and functional wall display.

STORAGE RACK

EQUIPMENT

Stiff wire brush
Coarse-grade wire wool
Electric hammer drill
Masonry drill bit
Screwdriver

MATERIALS

Galvanised wire letter basket
Four rawlpugs
Four 38 mm (1½ in) screws

METHOD

1 Make sure that the basket is dry and remove any remains of protective tape or packaging that might remain on it.

2 Clean the basket thoroughly with the stiff wire brush then finish with the wire wool to remove any residual oxidation or dirt.

When you are satisfied with the appearance of your basket, hold it up to the wall in the desired position, mark the fixing holes with a pencil, then drill the pencil-marked holes with the electric drill and masonry bit. Insert the rawlplugs before fixing the rack to the wall with the 38 mm (1½ in) screws.

Safety note

Rubber or protective gloves are recommended for this project.

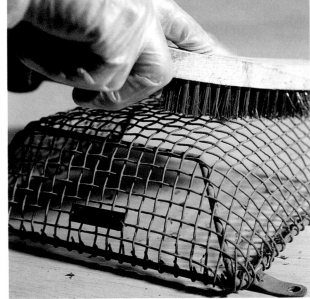

An easy answer to a constant storage problem – what to do with books, papers and all those other items that need to be close to hand but can clutter up the surface of a desk or table. A shelf is not always practicable and offers none of the advantages of the kind of storage that allows you to see instantly what is stored. A wall-mounted rack, however, offers useful vertical storage for any room in the house.

We located these woven, galvanised wire letter baskets in one of our favourite hunting grounds – government surplus yards. Made half a century ago for installation behind the doors of army married quarters, they had never been installed but were sold off and ignored until we found them. They had been stored out of doors, but the heavy galvanising had protected them from the degradation of years of exposure to the elements. Once retrieved and the remnants of the protective tape and brown paper packaging removed, they were almost as good as new.

We hope that this project will encourage you to look at unfamiliar objects with an open mind, because part of the enjoyment of working with salvaged materials is trying to think of new applications for them. When we first discovered these baskets, we thought that they were too good to miss though at the time we had no idea of what we might use them for. Once cleaned up, they have proved to be indispensable in helping to organise our office, the kitchen and our teenage daughter's bedroom.

SHUTTER CD RACK

We know from personal experience that this shutter CD rack is a good idea because it has a teenager's seal of approval. Teenagers usually buy CDs more frequently than the rest of us, and as a collection of CDs expands storage can become a problem.

Of the innumerable CD storage systems that are commercially available, most take up valuable surface space and few can be described as well designed. If, however, you are able to find an old wooden louvre shutter, which will undoubtedly need some attention, if only a coat of paint, we are sure you will agree that, once wall mounted at eye-level with the CD titles on view, it provides the ideal storage solution.

When selecting an old wooden shutter for conversion into a CD rack, make sure to measure the width of the slats and their distance apart to ensure that the finished rack will comfortably hold boxed CDs. If you wish, you can use the shutter in its original condition and not repaint it, but if it is to fit into an existing interior scheme it is probably best to paint it in the colour or colours of your choice. We selected an old shutter that showed considerable evidence of age and wear and decided to repaint it in two contrasting colours, completing it with a simulated aged and distressed finish.

EQUIPMENT

Screwdriver
Electric sander
Glasspaper
38 mm (1½ in) paintbrush
Soft cotton rag
Electric hammer drill
Masonry drill bit

MATERIALS

Old wooden window shutter
Colourless timber preservative
Wood filler (if necessary)
Two contrasting colours of matt emulsion
    paint
Satin finish interior wood varnish
Hardboard or thin plywood to fit the back
    of the shutter
Matt black emulsion paint
Small wood screws or panel pins
Two mirror plates
Rawlplugs
Screws to fit mirror plates

Safety note

We advise that you wear safety glasses or goggles when using any mechanical sanding equipment; a dust mask is also sensible in case the surface to be sanded has been finished with a lead-based paint. Rubber or protective gloves are also recommended for this project.

SHUTTER CD RACK

METHOD

1 Remove any hinges or other metal hardware, sand down any flaked and loose paint from the shutter and treat with colourless timber preservative. Fill any holes or damage with wood filler, wait for the filler to set then sand it down to match the surrounding timber. Sand the whole of the shutter to provide a smooth surface for repainting. It is not necessary to remove all the old paint, but pay particular attention to revealing the underlying timber on the edges of the frame and slats, where natural wear would occur.

2 When you are satisfied with the finish you have achieved, paint the shutter frame in the darker of your selected colours of emulsion paint and leave to dry. Then paint the slats in a contrasting paler colour and again leave to dry.

3 When the shutter is completely dry, sand through the surface of the paint to reveal the underlying wood on all the outside edges of the frame and the exposed edges of the slats. You can either use an electric sander or, for a more subtle effect, sand by hand. The sanding is designed to simulate natural wear; if you do make a mistake, it is very simple to repaint and start again.

4 When the frame is looking suitable distressed, clean off any dust with the cotton rag and apply two coats of satin finish interior wood varnish to the entire shutter, leaving it to dry between coats.

Cut the sheet of hardboard or thin plywood to fit approximately 12 mm (½ in) inside the reverse of the shutter. Paint one side with matt black emulsion and, when dry, attach it to the rear of the shutter with panel pins or screws. Fit two mirror plates to the rear of the shutter and decide on its hanging position. Drill the holes and insert rawlplugs before screwing the CD rack to the wall.

Fireplace designed by architect Mark Watson, cast in concrete moulded from an old milk churn discovered in the roof of this restored former stable, now a games room, and embellished with the original metal churn handles. The over-mantle was cut from 'green', air-dried oak.

The ideal kitchen these days is very much a living room, sometimes large enough to cook, eat and socialise in, making it the centre of family life. The sitting room and perhaps a

ROOMS FOR LIVING

conservatory are also rooms where family and friends can gather for informal entertaining, in tune with the more casual, relaxed lifestyle that many of us now choose.

The decor and the objects we display make a strong statement reflecting our personalities, and with the eclectic nature of decorating today, nothing is totally predictable. Mix surreal combinations of furniture and colours – that is half the fun of decorating. A favourite picture or object that costs next to nothing does not have to be taken too seriously, because it injects an individuality and freshness into a scheme that can easily be changed with the next new idea.

Salvage ideas for these living rooms include vintage office furniture, mass-produced between the 1930s and the 1960s, much of it made of steel or wood or a combination of both to be functional, durable and well designed. Now, after years of neglect, it is being reclaimed and restored, the dull grey paint covered with vibrant colours to give it a new lease of life, a new purpose and a place in our homes. Another unconventional idea, from Spanish furniture designer Diego Fortunato, is to make a base from the cheapest industrial metal shelving, once used to store plans, and to cover it with piles of huge, sumptuous velvet cushions in rich reds and purples, creating a stylish daybed.

These versatile pieces of furniture can be assimilated into any room, mixing comfortably with antiques, at a fraction of the price paid for similar styles from a designer range.

In complete contrast, if you have a liking for the warmth of wood looking naturally distressed, consider using old scaffold boards, disused railway sleepers, discarded fencing, floorboards and farmyard gates for making into large dining tables, coffee tables, benches, mirrors, picture frames and capacious cupboards. This rough-hewn, unrefined furniture celebrates its origins, revelling in the occasional evidence of woodworm, knots and scores in its often stained, battered and worn surfaces.

NEAR LEFT

A carved wooden fire surround, bought from a reclamation yard then gilded and fitted with glass, makes a superb over-mantle mirror above a drawing-room fireplace.

BOTTOM RIGHT

A decorative over-mantle has been painted and placed above a shelf in a laundry room to deflect the eye from the utilitarian boiler below.

BOTTOM LEFT

The unusual door was cut down and made to fit the opening to what was once the vestry of this converted church. The stone kitchen sink, taps and marble-top butcher's slab all came from a reclamation yard. The owner of the church once taught art courses, and the large plate seen behind the taps was a present from a ceramics student.

FAR LEFT

Cast-iron nineteenth-century pillars salvaged from a Baptist chapel make an elegant feature installed behind plate glass doors which lead on to a flag-stoned terrace and the well-managed garden beyond.

LEFT

The rack above the cooking range was at one time used to hang cassocks in the vestry, and the Victorian tiles were amassed over a period of twenty or thirty years by Angela Coombes, the owner of this converted church. The evocative framed photograph by Norman Parkinson was taken for *Queen* magazine in the Chanel showroom, Paris, in the early 1960s; it is part of the Angela Coombes archive collection.

SLATE-TILED WALL

EQUIPMENT

Palette knife
Emery paper or emery cloth
Tape measure
Diamond-blade electric tile cutter
Slate cutter (optional)
50 mm (2 in) paintbrush
Spirit level
Chalk
Tile adhesive spreader
Cotton rag
Fine artist's paintbrush

MATERIALS

Selection of old roofing slates
Black matt emulsion paint
Wall tile adhesive
Satin finish interior or floor varnish

Safety note

Electrical cutting equipment can be dangerous. Most electric tile cutters use water as a coolant and create a great deal of spray. You are advised to wear safety goggles if using any electrical cutter, and gloves and protective clothes are advisable if you use a water-cooled tile cutter.

Slate, limestone, terracotta and marble are immensely popular natural wall and floor coverings in both domestic and commercial environments, despite strong competition from modern man-made high-tech materials.

Hard-wearing slate has long been admired for its beauty as well as its durability. It comes in wonderful shades of red and heather blue as well as the classic dark blue-grey which seems to go with everything and has always been a favourite material for floors, kitchen worktops and wall cladding. A mix of slate with limestone, marble or terracotta is very much in vogue. Despite the fact that they are a fraction of the thickness of traditional flooring slate and have a tendency to flake, reclaimed roofing slates can be used very successfully on floors if laid on a bed of cement to give them a solid base. Floor tiles were often sealed with a coat of milk or oil in the days before pre-prepared sealants became readily available.

Select your old roofing slates for condition. Ideally those you use for this project should be fairly regular in thickness, free of too much flaking (delamination), of similar colour and should have two reasonably undamaged edges. If the tiles are in particularly good condition, there may be no need to cut them down, but most reclaimed slates have at least one edge damaged and the nail fixing holes have enlarged due to the passage of time and the enthusiasm with which they were removed from the roof.

SLATE-TILED WALL

METHOD

If the slates you will be using for this project are delaminating, it is a good idea to prise off the loose layers with a palette knife or similar blade until you have revealed a sound surface. This surface can be cleaned with emery paper or wetted emery cloth to produce a smooth finish.

Measure your tiles and decide on a size into which the tiles can be economically cut. This size should ensure that the cut slate will not include any unsightly nail holes and that the width will be trimmed to lose any damaged edge. For simplicity, we chose to cut our slates into squares, which has the advantage that cutting on the diamond-bladed tile cutter is accomplished in two passes with no need to change the saw fence setting.

Slates cut in this fashion will have two straight cut edges and two of the original naturally bevelled edges. For a really professional finish, you should make the first two cuts of the slate about 25 mm (1 in) larger than the required dimension, then reduce the saw fence measurement and pass the slates through the saw for a third and fourth time, trimming off the bevelled edges to give four neatly cut edges.

It is perfectly possible to cut the slates for this project with a slate cutter (see the Slate Table Mats project in the chapter Wining and Dining), but the resulting edges may not allow the cut slates to be butted neatly together.

1 Measure the area you will be tiling with the cut slates and work out the number required. Remember to provide for areas where slates will need to be cut to shape or where part-slates will be required for edges or ends of runs. We suggest that you cut a number of extra slates to provide for inevitable breakages.

Start the diamond-blade tile cutter and make sure that the water reservoir is full and that the spinning blade produces a fine spray of water to both lubricate and cool the slate when it is being cut. Set the fence to the desired width, hold the slate firmly in both hands and, with the true edge against the fence, pass it across the saw table until cut through. Turn the slate through 90 degrees and make a second cut at right angles to the first to produce a square slate with two cut and two bevelled edges. Repeat until you have as many slates as you require.

2 Carefully mark out the area you will be tiling and paint it with one or two coats of matt black emulsion paint. When the paint is dry, mark the central point on the width of the area to be tiled and, using a spirit level for accuracy, draw a line from the floor to the top of the area with chalk. Calculate how many horizontal rows of slates will be required to tile the area, halve that number and multiply by the dimension of the cut slates. Measure down from the top of the area to be tiled by this amount, and at that point draw a second and horizontal line crossing the first and stretching from one side of the area to the other.

3 Begin by fixing the slates as vertical and horizontal rows abutting the chalk marks, leaving a matchstick width between. Apply wall tile adhesive with the spreader to the back of a slate, then press it firmly on to the wall with a gentle twisting movement. Remove any excess adhesive with a damp cloth. For best results, as far as possible try to fit cut edge against cut edge and bevelled edge against bevelled edge. When you have fitted the slates to the chalk lines, commence filling in the remaining area with further slates, using the first rows as a guide, until the wall is covered. Periodically check your work with the spirit level and tape measure.

4 Use the slate cutter or the diamond-bladed tile cutter to trim slates to fit round awkward areas and where half- or part-slates are required. Use a moist rag to remove any spilled adhesive and wipe over the surface of the slates to remove any last residues of dirt or dust. When the adhesive is completely dry, use the fine artist's brush dipped in the black matt emulsion paint to touch up as required. Apply at least two coats of satin finish interior or floor varnish (the floor varnish is somewhat harder wearing), leaving the wall to dry between coats. Pay particular attention to covering those areas between the slates where the black paint is revealed.

To maintain the appearance of your slate-tiled wall, periodically wipe it over with a damp cloth. If the finish deteriorates, it can be restored with a further application of varnish.

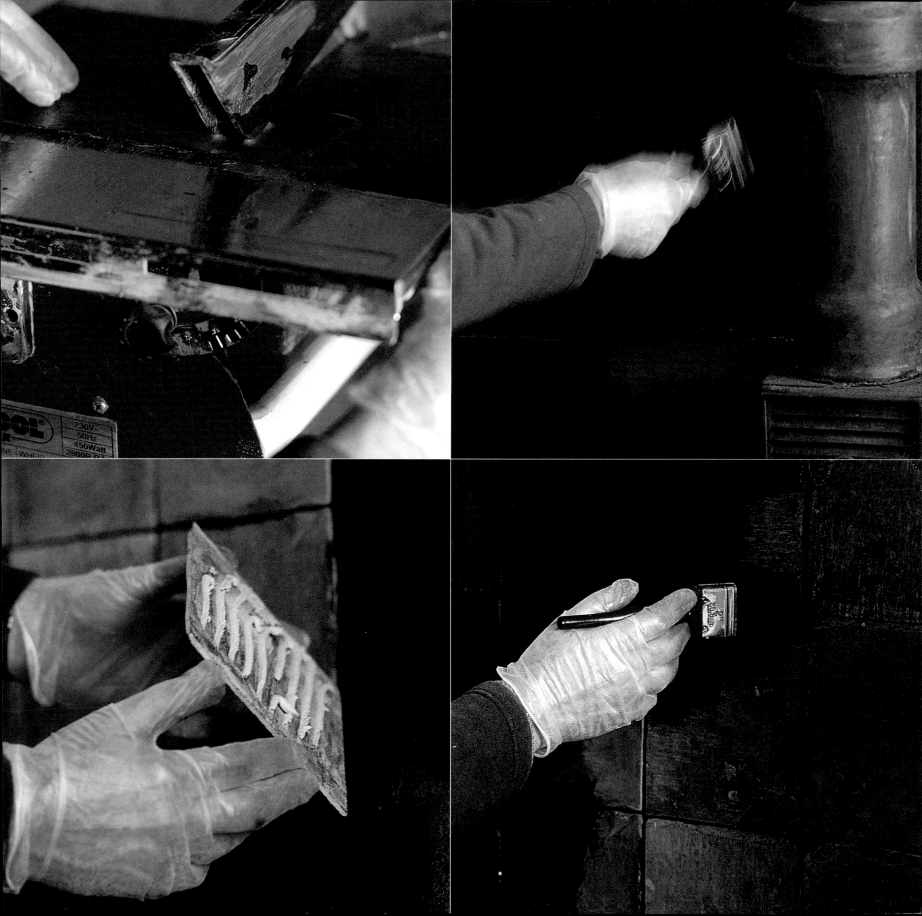

WAISTED CUPBOARD

EQUIPMENT

Bench saw or band saw
Tape measure
Set square
Hammer
Electric jigsaw
Saucer
Electric sander
Glasspaper
Electric drill and drill bit
Screwdriver
25 mm (1 in) paintbrush
Waxing brush or stiff-bristled paintbrush
Soft polishing brush
Lint-free cotton rag

MATERIALS

Waterproof wood glue
38 mm (1½ in) annular ring nails
38 mm (1½ in) panel pins
25 mm (1 in) panel pins
Mid-brown wood stain
Four 75 mm (3 in) screws
Antique brown furniture wax
18 mm (¾ in) brass screws
Two 65 mm (2½ in) brass Parliament or butt
  hinges
13 cm (5 in) brass pull handle
40 mm (1⅝ in) brass turn button
25 mm (1 in) brass screw and washer

Safety note

Protective glasses or goggles are essential if you
are using power cutting equipment and a dust
mask is advisable. Rubber or protective gloves are
also recommended for this project.

TIMBER

For the sides:
Four boards approx. 89 cm x 11 cm x
  12 mm (35 x 4¼ x ½ in)

For the shelves:
Three pieces of floorboard approx. 22 cm x
  22 mm (8½ x ⅞ in), one cut to 28 cm
  (11 in) and two cut to 30 cm (12 in)

For the back:
Four boards approx. 89 cm x 9 cm x 15 mm
  (35 x 3½ x ⅝ in)

For the front:
Two boards approx. 89 cm x 9 cm x 15 mm
  (35 x 3½ x ⅝ in)
One top piece approx. 17 cm x 9 cm x
  15 mm (6½ x 3½ x ⅝ in)
One bottom piece approx. 17 cm x 12.5 cm
  x 15 mm (6½ x 5 x ⅝ in)

For the door:
Two boards approx. 63 cm x 85 mm x
  15 mm (24¾ x 3¼ x ⅝ in)
Two braces approx. 17 cm x 10 cm x
  15 mm (6½ x 4 x ⅝ in)
Two pieces approx. 17 cm x 15 mm x
  15 mm (6½ x ⅝ x ⅝ in)

For the top:
Two pieces to make approx. 38 x 26 x 5 cm
  (15 x 10¼ x 2 in)

Other:
You will also need a number of pieces of
waste timber for bracing and supporting
the joints.

If you are looking for furniture or storage ideas with some individuality – something a little different from the mass-produced designs of the high street – try making our rustic-looking 'waisted' cupboard. This highly unusual, 'semi-rough' cupboard can be made in all sorts of sizes, and we have made a very successful taller version. It was constructed using timber salvaged from horticultural and produce boxes, some with the original stencil marking intact, imported from the Netherlands into Britain before the use of lighter-weight cardboard and plastic containers. Had it not been rescued, this timber would have been used for firewood.

Select different thicknesses of wood for the construction: thin for the sides without knots (to allow for uniform bending into the 'waist' shape), thicker for the doors, front and back, and thicker still for the interior shelves. Any piece of waste timber can be used for the top of the cupboard, as long as it is fairly chunky. We cut our front, door and sides from the framework of the horticultural boxes, whilst the sides were made from the thinner cladding. The shelves were sawn from an old floorboard and the top was cut from two pieces of old floor joist, glued together to create a piece of the required width. We waxed the finished piece and used 'aged' brass door fittings, but it could also be given a very effective naturally distressed limed look and fitted with old steel hinges, handle and turn button.

WAISTED CUPBOARD

METHOD

This project demonstrates how to make a waisted cupboard measuring approximately 94 cm (37 in) high x 26 cm (10¼ in) deep and 38 cm (15 in) wide. All measurements can be adjusted to make a cupboard of a different size.

1 Cut the four pieces of timber cut the sides of the cupboard, making sure that there are few knots in the timber, and measure three points 75 mm (3 in), 42 cm (16½ in) and 76 cm (30 in) from one end (the top). Use the set square and a pencil to mark lines at these points across the width of the boards. Apply wood glue to the ends of the three shelves and nail them to the side pieces at these points, using the 38 mm (1½ in) annular ring nails to hold the joints securely. The 28 cm (11 in) shelf should be nailed at the 42 cm (16½ in) point to form the middle shelf.

2 Turn the assembled framework on to its front, keeping the unsawn and naturally coloured edge of the shelves facing the front of the cupboard, then, with a pencil, mark a point at the exact centre of the width of each shelf. Apply wood glue to approximately the central 18 cm (7 in) of the rear of each shelf and use 38 mm (1½ in) panel pins to secure one of the four back boards to the shelves so that one edge exactly abuts each marked centre point. (This will ensure that the curved sides match.) Place a second board abutting and outside the first one, and secure it lightly in place with just one or two 25 mm (1 in) panel pins.

3 Attach the third and fourth back boards in the same way to the opposite side of the centre marks. Turn the frame over so that the back of the cupboard is underneath and the extra width of the newly fitted boards can be seen protruding from under the curved edges. With a pencil, draw the shape of the curve on these boards, again turn the frame over, remove the loosely fitted two outside boards and extract the panel pins used to fit them temporarily in place.

4 Place the two removed boards on a solid work surface and cut out the pencil-marked curve with the jigsaw. Apply wood glue to the rear of the shelves and fit the two cut-out back boards in position with 38 mm (1½ in) panel pins.

5 Turn the cupboard on to its back and mark the shelf centres on the front with a pencil. Mark a point 85 mm (3¼ in) away on either side of these centre marks on each shelf. Place one of the 89 cm (35 in) front boards abutting the outside of these points and secure it with one or two 25 mm (1 in) panel pins. Turn the cupboard over, mark the curve with a pencil, remove the board and cut out the shape with the jigsaw. Apply wood glue to the front of the shelves where the board was placed and fit in position with 38 mm (1½ in) panel pins. Repeat with the second front board.

6 Take the 17 cm x 9 cm x 15 mm (6½ x 3½ x ⅝ in) front top piece, apply glue to the sides and the exposed edge of the top shelf of the cupboard, then nail the top piece securely in place between the curved front boards with 38 mm (1½ in) panel pins, its top flush with the top of the cupboard. (It may be necessary to support this piece with scrap timber glued and nailed with 25 mm/1 in panel pins behind the curved front boards.) The 17 cm x 12.5 cm x 15 mm (6½ x 5 x ⅝ in) front bottom piece should be fitted to the bottom of the cupboard between the curved front boards, supported by scrap timber glued and nailed from behind with 25 mm (1 in) panel pins. When the glue has dried, place a saucer or similar circular shape at the base of the fitted bottom piece, draw round the curve with a pencil and cut out with the jigsaw.

7 Use the electric sander and glasspaper to smooth off all irregularities, sharp corners and rough timber. Stain any sawn edges with mid-brown wood stain, diluted to match the existing weathered timber. Measure the door space you have created and put the cupboard to one side. Take the two 63 cm (24¾ in) door boards and join them together with the two 17 cm (6½ in) braces fitted across the rear and fixed with wood glue and 25 mm (1 in) panel pins. Take the two 17 cm (6½ in) pieces of 15 mm (⅝ in) square timber, glue one side and fit one each to the top and bottom of the door with 38 mm (1½ in) panel pins. This will help to prevent the door cupping (distorting). Place the assembled door in position and shape with the electric sander to fit it loosely in place.

8 Glue and nail four pieces of waste timber above the top shelf, inside and flush with the top of the cupboard, to provide a base into which the screws used to fit the top will be fixed. When the glue is dry, apply more wood glue to the top of the waste timber and place the two pieces forming the top in place, the back flush with the rear of the cupboard and with an equal overhang on each side. Drill four holes through the top into the waste timber underneath and fix in place with 75 mm (3 in) screws.

Use the waxing brush or soft-bristled paintbrush to apply antique brown furniture wax to the door, top, front and sides of the cupboard. When it is dry, polish with the soft brush and lint-free cotton rag. Use the 18 mm (¾ in) brass screws to fit the brass hinges to the door, centred 15 cm (6 in) from the top and bottom. Finally, attach the brass pull handle and fit the turn button outside the door with a 25 mm (1 in) brass screw and a washer underneath, positioned so that it will secure the door when closed.

CURTAIN POLE AND CURTAINS

EQUIPMENT

Tape measure
Hacksaw or pipe cutter
Paint stripper
Old paintbrush
Offcut of waste timber
Cotton rag
Craft knife
Glasspaper
Electric hammer drill
Masonry drill bit
Screwdriver

MATERIALS

Length of 25/28 mm (metric) copper tubing
Approx. 30 cm (12 in) broom handle
Two tent pole finials or similar decorative
    finials
Wood glue
Four brass 28 mm (metric) Munson rings
Four rawlplugs
Four 50 mm (2 in) screws
Clip-on brass curtain rings
Two antique linen sheets

Safety note

Paint stripper is extremely caustic; rubber or protective gloves and eye protection are essential for this project.

It is so simple and inexpensive to make a curtain pole, given some old copper piping, two wooden tent pole finials and a few other bits and pieces, that you may decide never to buy one again. Just think of the savings if you were you to make them for the whole house!

Copper piping develops colour and patination with age even when the metal is hidden behind layers of paint. It can be bought second-hand from a waste metal merchant who will probably charge you for the scrap value only. Copper pipe can be found in various gauges and we chose 25/28mm (metric) for our curtain pole, a gauge often still used in internal pipe work.

To fix the pipe to the wall we used Munson rings, which are purpose-made for pipe fixing. They are manufactured in two parts: the bracket has two screw holes to allow it to be fixed to the wall, whilst the outer part which screws into the bracket comprises two semi-circular holders which secure the pipe. Munson rings are readily available, inexpensive and provide a practical alternative to curtain brackets.

The metal pipe and wood fittings combine well for the casual, unsophisticated look we were aiming for. We teamed the pole with simple curtains of heavy antique cream linen. Essentially utilitarian, sometimes embroidered with initials in red and occasionally fringed, they were used as sheets in French farmhouses in the early 1900s. Those we used were particularly long and had one embroidered and tasselled end. We chose to make a feature of this by folding and hanging them so that the embroidery could be seen.

CURTAIN POLE AND CURTAINS

METHOD

1 Measure the width of the window opening for which the curtain pole is being made. Add approximately 20 cm (8 in) at each end, then cut the copper tube to that dimension with a pipe cutter or hacksaw. If the pipe is painted, strip the paint with chemical paint stripper. Follow the manufacturer's instructions carefully and use protective gloves, eye protection and wear an apron or old clothes when doing this. Lay the pipe on a disposable surface and apply the stripper liberally to the painted surface with an old paintbrush. Leave for a short while until the paint blisters, then start to remove the softened paint with a scrap of waste wood. Do not use a metal scraper or anything else that is likely to scratch the surface of the pipe and so remove the patination that has developed over time. Repeat the process as many times as is necessary to remove all the paint, wiping the pipe clean with cotton rag between applications.

2 When the pipe is clean, wash it down with soapy water, dry with clean cotton rag and place to one side. Cut the broom handle into two halves with the hacksaw. Using the craft knife and glasspaper, shape and sand down an end of one until it fits tightly into one of the tent pole finials. Fit the other piece of broom handle into the second finial in the same way. Use the craft knife and glasspaper to shape and sand the other ends: one finial should fit tightly into the pipe, whilst the other should be sanded so that it is slightly loose and can be easily removed to allow the curtain rings to be fitted over the pipe.

3 Place the completed curtain pole against and above the window in the desired position and mark where the supports should be fitted. These should be placed at both ends of the pole and just outside the window opening, leaving an approximately 15 cm (6 in) overhang at each end. Unscrew the Munson rings from their brackets, place the brackets at the selected points on the wall and mark the screw holes with a pencil. Drill out holes in the wall at the marked points with the electric drill and masonry bit to a depth of approximately 50 mm (2 in), insert the rawlplugs and fit the Munson ring brackets with the four 50 mm (2 in) screws.

Unscrew the two semi-circular Munson ring holders and attach the halves with the threaded attachment to the brackets fixed to the wall.

4 Remove the loose finial from one end of the pole, thread the curtain rings on to it and replace the finial. Offer up the pole to the half Munson rings attached to the brackets and secure it in place with the previously removed half-rings. Check that the pole is centred on the brackets and, importantly, that one curtain ring is positioned outside the bracket but inside the finial on each side. Secure in place, tightening the Munson ring bolts with the screwdriver.

Fold the sheets so that, when hung, they will drop to the ground. Divide the curtain rings in two, push half to each end of the pole for each curtain and clip them on to the folded material at regular intervals. The last ring on each side, positioned outside the bracket, will keep the curtains spread when they are pulled across the window.

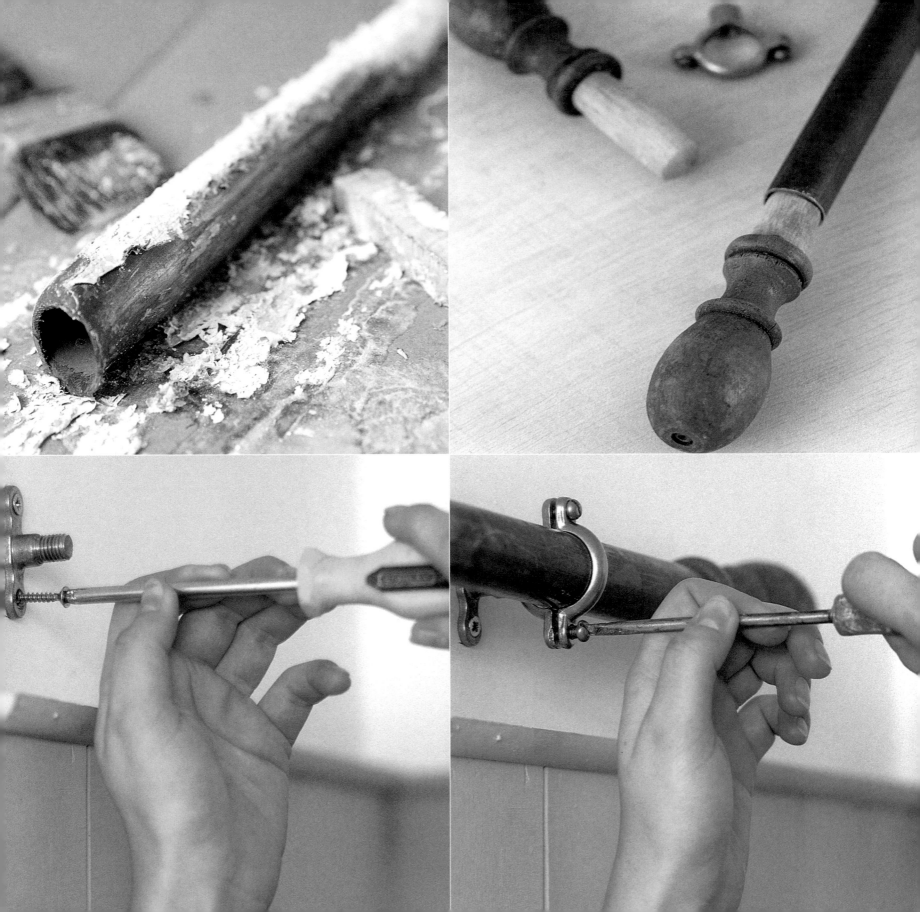

SEA DEFENCE COFFEE TABLE

EQUIPMENT

Angle grinder and sanding disc attachment
Orbital electric sander
Waxing brush or stiff-bristled paintbrush
Lint-free cotton rag
Kitchen paper (optional)

MATERIALS

Three wood blocks
Dark brown furniture wax
Glass round at least 12 mm (½ in) thick
Glass cleaner

METHOD

1 Select three blocks that match in appearance and height. If the ends are not level, they should be sawn or sanded to shape. Place one of the wooden blocks on a flat work surface covered with a disposable surface. Use the angle grinder to grind off any surface irregularities and heavy saw marks and finish to a smooth surface with the orbital sander.

2 Apply a liberal quantity of dark brown furniture wax to the sides and top of the block with the waxing or stiff-bristled brush. Rub the wax well into the surface with the soft cotton rag to accentuate the grain and colour of the timber; rub off any excess and leave it to dry. Be careful not to apply any wax to the base of the block because this will mark the floor when the coffee table is installed.

3 Polish with some lint-free cotton rag, using a new cloth when the first is soiled. For best results, polishing should be done in a figure of eight motion, which should leave no smears or marks on the surface of the wood. Be careful to remove any surface wax from the sawn surface of the top of the block because this might mark the glass top. Again, check the base of the block for any wax residue.

Place the three blocks carefully in the place where you propose to install the coffee table. The blocks should be placed an equal distance from each other and so that their tops will be approximately 20 cm (8 in) from the outside edge of the glass when it is placed on top. Clean the glass with glass cleaner, polishing it with more lint-free cotton rag or absorbent kitchen paper, and, when you are satisfied with the result, gently place the glass in position on the blocks.

Safety note

When using an angle grinder it is advisable to use safety glasses or goggles and a dust mask. A dust mask should always be used when sanding with an electric sander. Rubber or protective gloves are also recommended for this project.

When our eyes first alighted on
the massive wooden blocks cut
from the tapered ends of old oak
sea defence supports, we were
immediately drawn to their size
and streng░░░ese timbers, lifted
from the sea bed when the
defences were renewed, were
rescued by John Tyler of JAT
Reclamation, who cut them into
beams and lintels, leaving behind
the tapered ends which we
discovered in his yard.

Years of exposure to salt water
had hardened and darkened the
oak, which had also been
discoloured by the iron nails
driven in to fix the steel caps
that once protected them.

We felt strongly that these
chunks of raw timber could be
turned into something exciting
and innovative, and decided on a
design for a coffee table using the
posts for legs░ By chance, we
came across a huge salvaged
round of glass, so heavy that it
took two men to lift it. The origins
of this junk shop find were
unknown, but our hunch was that
it had previously been used as a
table top, suffering remarkably
few scratches. The combination
of gleaming glass and natural
warm, tactile wood gave us
exactly the clean architectural
lines and interesting contours we
had envisaged.

Any timber blocks could be
used to make a similar table, or
you may wish to construct the
legs from terracotta pipes, lumps
of stone or even concrete blocks.

SEA DEFENCE LAMP

EQUIPMENT

Electric drill
12 mm (½ in) spade or auger bit
Drill bit extension bar
Poker (optional)
Tenon saw
12 mm (½ in) wood chisel
Hacksaw
Metal file
Palette knife
Electrician's screwdriver
Stiff-bristled brush (optional)
Soft cotton rag (optional)

MATERIALS

Oak post or other large block of wood
30 cm (12 in) of 10 mm (metric)
    threaded brass batten
Threaded brass lamp holder
Threaded brass adaptor (optional)
Two-part epoxy putty
Approx. 20 cm (8 in) of 15 mm (⅝ in)
    copper tube
Fused electric plug
Three-wire lamp cord
Brown sealant or filler
Antique brown furniture wax (optional)
Lampshade cradle
Electric light bulb
Lampshade

Safety note

Electricity is potentially dangerous; we suggest you get a qualified and experienced electrician to check any electrical work you undertake for this project. Since a metal lamp fitting is used for this lamp, it is most important that three-wire lamp cord is used and that the earth wire is connected both to the lamp holder and the fused electrical plug.

Rough-hewn and shaped like obelisks, these mighty, metal-braced, oak sea defence posts, once driven deep into the tidal sands to support the palisades that protect the coast from sea erosion, were a truly exciting discovery. Because of their singularity, we felt that they were more than worthy of two different treatments. In this project, one has been made into a lamp with something of an oriental feel, and the shade reinforces the shape of the rich, dark, heavy base. The alternative project (Sea Defence Coffee Table on the previous pages) uses three posts as gargantuan legs for an ethnically stylish glass-topped coffee table.

SEA DEFENCE LAMP

METHOD

1 Place the wooden block on a flat surface, mark the centre point on the top surface and drill a hole to the maximum depth possible, making sure the electric drill is held vertically. Either remove the drill, attach the bit to an extension bar and continue drilling until you have drilled through to the bottom of the block, or turn the block over and drill from the base to meet the hole drilled from the top.

2 Should you choose to drill from each end and the holes do not quite meet, or you need to deepen a drilled hole, you can heat a poker until its tip is red hot and use it to burn through the remaining timber. This may require several applications of the poker and will create considerable smoke. We suggest that you undertake this job out of doors and make sure that the block does not catch fire. Have some water handy.

3 Use the tenon saw to make two cuts approximately 12 mm (½ in) apart and 12 mm (½ in) deep on the base of the block from the central hole to an outside edge. Chisel out the waste to form a groove for the lamp cord. Place the length of 10 mm threaded batten in a vice or on a bench hook and cut it to length with a hacksaw. Clean the cut end with a metal file and test that it will thread easily on to the lamp holder. Depending on the thread gauges of the batten and lamp holder used, it may be necessary to join them with a threaded brass adapter.

4 Insert the batten into the hole cut through the wooden block, securing it in place with two-part epoxy putty or a similar filler or glue. Make sure that the batten is vertical in the hole and that no putty will prevent the lamp cord being threaded through the batten and through the hole drilled in the block. Use a palette knife to clean the top of the block of any putty squeezed out when the batten was inserted, then put the block to one side for the putty to harden.

5 Screw the lamp holder on to the batten. Measure from the top of the block to the base of the lamp holder and cut the 15 mm (⅝ in) copper tube to that length. Unscrew the lamp holder. Fit a fused electric plug to one end of the lamp cord, place the copper tube over the batten to form a sleeve, then pass the free end of the cord up through the base of the wooden block and through the batten until it emerges from the top. Fit the cord to the lamp holder with an electrician's screwdriver, then pull it back through the block until the lamp holder sits on top of the batten and copper pipe. Screw the lamp holder back on to the batten, securing the copper pipe sleeve in position.

Use the brown sealant or filler to secure the lamp cord into the groove cut into the base of the block. At this point, the lamp base may be waxed with antique brown furniture wax applied with the stiff-bristled brush, rubbed into the wood with soft cotton rag and polished off with more rag. Fit a lampshade frame on to the collar of the lamp holder, insert a light bulb and place your selected lampshade on the frame.

As we start the new millennium with a softer look, a more gentle kind of minimalism, we use decorative accessories to add impact and interest. Pottery, paintings, porcelain, cushions, less-worn areas of an old rug can be cut up and backed with sacking material to make enormous floor cushions or wall hangings, and the offcuts can be used for smaller cushions.

DECORATIVE ACCESSORIES

rugs and cherished collections that have evolved over time are the clever touches that transform a furnished house into a warm, welcoming and comfortable home. Not all decorative accessories need be expensive, and when you are bored with something cheap and cheerful, the look can easily be changed.

Textiles bring life and colour to a room. Use large throws and rugs, especially vegetable-dyed kilims in soft natural shades. The

Antique quilt covers, faded linens and silk saris, fabrics and colours in exquisite textures can be mixed to give a vibrant new look to jaded interiors. Visit jumble sales and bric-à-brac shops or raid the attic to find tapestries and beautiful brocades that were once much-loved curtains or ball gowns, which you can cut up to create sumptuous soft furnishings. Salvage old embroideries, braids, trimmings, fringes and ribbons for added decoration.

LEFT

Broken pieces of china and odd cup handles make up this vibrant mosaic vase, which is an early piece by Candace Bahouth.

RIGHT

This display of kitchen utensils, including various food graters collected from all over Europe, makes a focal point that is decorative as well as practical.

FAR RIGHT

Too worn for everyday use, these vegetable-dyed kilims have been salvaged and turned into beautiful floor cushions, their subtle colours blending with existing furnishings.

We show comfortable cushions made from old velvet curtains in delicious jewel-like colours with contrast piping, and the same vibrant colours used to recover outdated ottomans, finished off with a silk tassel.

Plain walls can be effectively decorated with framed pictures skilfully hung. Old floorboard timbers and disused scaffold boards are an obvious choice to make mirror or picture frames, the larger they are the more dramatic the effect. Do not dismiss the subtle black/brown tar finish of salvaged shiplap timber, disfigured and rotting former fencing posts or abandoned five-bar farm gates. Even prickly hedgerow twigs, berries and small boughs, glued together on to a small wooden frame and painstakingly gilded, make the most imaginative of frames.

Slate roofing tiles can be cut to suitable sizes to make frames or table mats, and discarded decorative windows, once a source of light and ventilation, can be transformed into unusual and imaginative mirrors by removing the panes and making use of the frames. Next time you dig the garden, start collecting all those fragments of pretty broken china found buried beneath the surface and turn them into a mosaic table top or cover a small shelf, an urn or a lamp base. A visit to the beach could be the start of a shell or pebble collection to cover small items like frames or boxes, turning them into intriguing decorative accessories.

Metals of different descriptions, from blackened iron curtain poles to the gleaming modernity of zinc, have been enjoying an upsurge in popularity for the past few years. Metal looks good on its own but mixes equally well with the natural textures of wood, stone, slate and terracotta. It is often used in kitchens and bathrooms because of its hardwearing and practical qualities, but it should not be excluded from other rooms in the house. Tin plate is an inexpensive alternative to zinc with a strong contemporary look. So hunt out old catering tins: cleaned up, they can easily and inexpensively be adapted to make attractive, gleaming window boxes for herbs or flowers.

Books that are read and enjoyed give a home a lived-in, comfortable feel, and vases of freshly cut flowers, admired for their sweet-smelling scent as much as their beauty, can fill every room in the house.

LEFT

A glorious flight of fancy from Porter Design. Hedgerow cuttings have been dried, hot-glued to a wooden frame, sprayed with gesso and finished with solid gold leaf.

BOTTOM LEFT

Rich velvet curtains have been made into cushions by Milo Design. Enough fabric was left to cover an old ottoman.

FAR LEFT

A mirror made from roofing slates screwed on to a plywood base shows how basic materials can be given a new lease of life.

TONGUE-AND-GROOVE CLOCK

EQUIPMENT

Tape measure
Handsaw
Craft knife (optional)
Glasspaper
Mitre saw
Electric drill
Drill bit to fit the housing nut on the
    clock shaft
Hammer
Pliers

MATERIALS

Selection of tongue-and-groove
    match-boarding
Square of 9 mm (⅜ in) or 12 mm (½ in)
    plywood
Wood glue
25 mm (1 in) panel pins
Length of rough-cut timber approx.
    50 x 12 mm (2 x ½ in)
Battery-driven clock
Battery

METHOD

1 Choose a variety of different coloured tongue-and-groove match-boarding for similarity in size and pattern. Remove the tongue from the selected boards with a handsaw or craft knife, and finish flush with the edge with glasspaper to match the opposite grooved side. To cut the equilateral triangular pieces for your clockface, measure the width of the board and make a mark that distance along one length of the board for each two pieces you wish to cut. Cut off one end of the board at the first mark with the 90 degree setting of the mitre saw, move the saw to the 45 degree position and cut out the triangle. When the first triangle is cut, move the saw back to the 90 degree setting, slide the board up to the next mark and cut out a second triangle. Continue until you have cut the number of triangles required. Repeat with the different coloured boards.

2 Arrange the cut triangles on a flat surface until you have created the pattern you think looks most attractive. Measure the outside dimensions and cut a square to that size from the 9 mm (⅜ in) or 12 mm (½ in) plywood. Apply wood glue to one face of the plywood and place the triangles on it in your chosen pattern.

Place a weight on top and put to one side to dry. When it is fully dry, place the clock face up on a piece of waste timber and drill a hole in the centre from the front through the boarding and plywood and into the waste wood underneath. Drilling through the face into waste wood minimises the risk of the hole tearing where the bit emerges.

3 Take the length of rough-cut timber and cut it on the mitre saw to fit as a frame around the clockface. Fix it in place with wood glue and 25 mm (1 in) panel pins driven into the plywood edges.

4 Fit the clock housing nut from the front into the hole drilled into the clockface, then insert the clock mechanism from the rear, passing the shaft up through the drilled hole into the housing nut. Attach the clock hands and secure with the locking nut tightened with pliers. Attach a battery to the reverse of the clock mechanism, adjust the hands to the correct time and hang your finished clock in place. If you wish, you can fit a strut to the rear of the clock and use it free-standing.

We much admired frames made from recycled tongue-and-groove cypress match-boarding on the stand of Laville Frames Inc. at a furniture trade fair in North Carolina. Thomas and Ursula Laville run a business in Baton Rouge, Louisiana, committed to 'ecological consciousness'. They make an ever-widening range of furniture from salvaged and recycled materials, including rusted corrugated iron, copper sheet, pine skirting boards and other discarded timbers.

In this project we show how a simple clock can be constructed from readily sourced tongue-and-groove match-boarding.

Tongue-and-groove match-boarding has been produced in a multitude of sizes and patterns. Modern tongue-and-groove, sold as 'T&G', is generally about 100 mm (4 in) in width and 6 mm (¼ in) in thickness; older tongue-and-groove can be 15 cm (6 in), 20 cm (8 in) or even 23 cm (9 in) wide and is normally 12 mm (½ in) thick. Various patterns are available, the most common is tongue, groove and vee or 'TG&V', and the most attractive is probably tongue, groove and bead, 'TG&Bead'. When butted together, the tongue of each board fits into the groove of its neighbour, and the vee or bead makes an attractive and uniform feature across the assembled boarding.

Much salvaged tongue-and-groove is damaged in the process of being dismantled, often having its tongue broken off, but since this project calls for the tongue to be removed anyway, this damaged timber, which can often be purchased quite cheaply, is fine.

FENCE FRAME

EQUIPMENT

Tape measure
Set square
Handsaw
Screwdriver
Medium-grade glasspaper
12 mm (½ in) paintbrush
Glass cleaner
Lint-free cotton rag or kitchen paper
Hammer
Electric hammer drill (optional)
Masonry drill bit (optional)

MATERIALS

Two 135 cm (53 in) lengths of 12 mm (½ in)
    thick fence timber, one 75 mm (3 in)
    wide and one 65 mm (2½ in) wide,
    selected for colour and condition
Colourless wood preservative
Wood glue
18 mm (¾ in) screws
Medium brown timber stain
Glass or mirror glass to fit frame rebate
Hardboard or 6 mm (¼ in) plywood to fit
    frame rebate
25 mm (1 in) panel pins
Two screw eyes or D rings
Picture hook or screw hook
Nylon picture cord

Safety note

Remember always to use a wall
fixing able to hold the weight of
your frame. Smaller frames can
be securely hung on single or
double picture hooks which can
be driven into most plaster or
solid walls; heavier frames will
need to be hung on a hook
drilled and rawlplugged into
the wall.

METHOD

1 Treat your fence timber lengths with the wood preservative. Use a set square and pencil to mark the 75 mm (3 in) length into two 45 cm (18 in) and two 20 cm (8 in) lengths. Cut to length with the handsaw and, selecting the better face of the timber to be the front, place face down on a flat surface, with the shorter lengths placed between the longer lengths in the shape of the frame you are constructing.

2 Measure the width of the assembled frame shape. The measurement should be approximately 35 cm (14 in). Cut two pieces from the 65 mm (2½ in) fence timber to this length. Apply wood glue to the back of the assembled frame, then place the new timbers over both widths, making sure the outside edges match. Fix each length in place with 18 mm (¾ in) screws, ensuring that they are driven into all three lengths of underlying timber. Measure the gap between the two newly fitted lengths – the measurement should be approximately 33 cm (13 in) – and cut two lengths to that size from the remaining 65 mm (2½ in) fence timber. Fit these lengths into place on the frame, securing them with 18 mm (¾ in) screws, again ensuring that the outside edges are flush.

3 When the glue is dry, turn the assembled frame over and use glasspaper to sand off any sharp edges. Apply the medium brown stain, diluted to match, to disguise all the exposed newly sawn timber. Cut the glass or mirror glass (or have it cut by a glazier) and the hardboard or plywood backing to fit the frame rebate (approximately 33 x 23 cm/13 x 9 in). Clean the glass or mirror glass. Place your selected image between the cleaned glass and the backing and insert it into the frame; secure with 25 mm (1 in) panel pins driven into the sides of the rebate. Alternatively, place the mirror into the frame rebate and secure in the same way.

Measure approximately one-third down from the top of the frame and insert the screw eyes or D rings in the centre of each side of the frame. Pass the nylon cord through both rings, bring to the centre and tie securely with a slip-proof knot. Your frame or mirror is now ready to hang.

The wood used to frame this botanical print is rather appropriately taken from old garden fencing that had been dismantled and replaced. After years of battering from high winds, much had fallen down and some had rotted, but there was still an abundance of good solid wood that was reusable and consequently salvaged. Fencing is generally made from standard softwood but sometimes cedar is used, which has a natural resistance to rot. The uneven colour comes from exposure to the elements and the effects of lichens and fungi, which have attached themselves to the rough surface of the timber over the years.

Whether you are making mirror or picture frames, consider using reclaimed shiplap timber, old packing cases or pallets, all of which make interesting, unusual and inexpensive framing materials. The cost of having a number of pictures professionally mounted and framed can be prohibitive, whereas making your own is a satisfying alternative.

In this project we demonstrate how to make a frame measuring approximately 45 x 35 cm (18 x 14 in) overall, with an image size of approximately 30 x 20 cm (12 x 8 in). Obviously, you may construct a frame of almost any size, perhaps to fit a chosen picture or photograph, in which case the measurements must be adjusted accordingly. If you wish, this frame can be made as a mirror rather than a picture frame.

BREAD TIN PLANTER

EQUIPMENT

Medium-grade wire wool
12 mm (½ in) paintbrush
White spirit for brush cleaning

MATERIALS

Metal bread tin
Red oxide primer paint
Spray can of silver paint

METHOD

1 Although the tins had been stacked outdoors, the metallic plating was largely intact, except on the sides where they had been exposed to the weather. Rather than strip and laboriously polish the whole tin, we decided to treat the rust and refinish with silver metal paint. There are a number of silver metal paints currently available, but few accurately simulate a plated finish. The most convincing and effective we found are those produced for the automobile trade, which are available from car accessory shops.

2 Use the medium-grade wire wool to remove the surface rust and reveal a smooth metal substrate. Be careful to work along the length of the tin in order to minimise any unsightly scratching.

3 When you are satisfied with the finish you have achieved, apply one coat of red oxide paint to both the outside and inside of the tin with the paintbrush and leave to dry. Clean the brush with white spirit.

4 Read the manufacturer's directions on the spray paint carefully then, following their instructions, spray one coat of paint on the whole of the exterior of the tin and approximately 25 mm (1 in) down the inside. Be careful not to overspray and cause the paint to drip or sag. Put the tin to one side to dry.

When the paint is dry, the tin can be filled with potting compost and planted. The bread tin has no drainage holes, so plants must be watered from the top. Be careful not to overwater the plants and so cause the potting compost to become waterlogged.

Safety note

Rubber or protective gloves are recommended for this project. Work on a surface protected with newspaper or other disposable covering. Always use spray paints in a dust-free and well-ventilated area, and be careful not to breathe in fumes; we advise you to use a face mask.

Good-looking planters are not always easy to find, but this tin-plated planter filled with pots of pretty flowers or herbs is a wonderful way to smarten up your window sill with a bright, modern look.

The bread tins we found for this project had apparently been made in the 1960s, when industrial action in the baking industry threatened a bread shortage and the nation was being prepared to bake its own bread. Unfortunately, these tins, made by government order, proved too large for the average household oven, and of the thousands made all but a few were scrapped.

DOORSTOP

EQUIPMENT

Handsaw
Electric drill
16 mm (⅝ in) spade or auger drill bit
Hacksaw
Small palette knife
Waxing brush or stiff-bristled paintbrush
Lint-free soft cotton rag

MATERIALS

20 cm (8 in) piece of oak moulding
Two-part epoxy putty (or similar hard-hold
   filler)
Wrought-iron handle
Clear furniture wax

METHOD

1 Trim the end of the oak block to size with the handsaw. Place it on a work surface and drill a hole into the centre to approximately half its depth with the electric drill and spade or auger bit. Remove any sawdust or shavings from the drilled hole.

2 Mix the epoxy putty according to the manufacturer's instructions and place it in the drilled hole. Use the hacksaw to cut the handle shaft to fit the block, then insert it into the filled hole. Remove any excess putty that has been squeezed out with the palette knife. Make sure that the handle is standing upright; put to one side for the putty to set.

   Apply a coat of clear furniture wax to the top, sides and end (but not the bottom) with the waxing brush or stiff-bristled paintbrush and rub it into the wood with the soft cotton rag. When it is dry, polish it with more clean cotton rag.

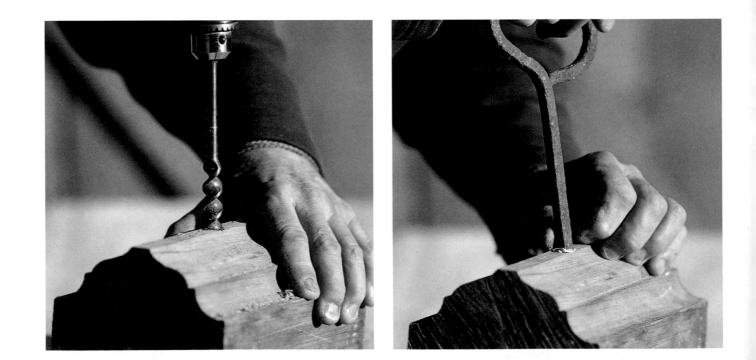

Unpretentious, this chamfered, golden oak offcut doorstop with a rusty iron door bolt handle, has plenty of rustic charm. The chunky 'green' oak moulded ceiling beam from which it was cut came from the restoration of a seventeenth-century manor house, and the rusty iron door bolt handle was found in our neglected farmhouse kitchen garden. The individual components of the doorstop appear most unpromising, but when assembled the finished doorstop has been much admired. Any number of things can be used to make similar doorstops, and the use of the epoxy putty, which provides a very strong hold, allows numerous different materials to be used. Consider using a nicely rounded stone or large pebble found during a day's beachcombing, with a hole drilled out for the handle, or any pleasing object that has enough weight to hold a door open when spring breezes whip through open windows, blowing the curtains and dislodging the cobwebs.

WINDOW MIRROR

EQUIPMENT

Stiff-bristled paintbrush
Paint stripper
Paint scraper
Wire brush (metal)
Medium-grade glasspaper (wood)
Small stiff brush (an old toothbrush is ideal)
Soft cotton rag
Soft polishing brush
Tape measure
Straight edge
Wax pencil or felt marker (to mark glass)
Glass cutter
Mastic gun (metal)
Light glazing hammer (wood)
Putty knife (wood)
Pliers

MATERIALS

Clear furniture wax
Antique brown furniture wax (wood)
2 mm (¹⁄₁₆ in) or 4 mm (³⁄₁₆ in) mirror glass
Brown mastic (metal)
Glazing putty (wood)
Glazing pins (wood)
Screw eyes or fitting lugs (metal)
Heavy-duty picture wire
Pair of mirror plates (wood)

Safety note

Be careful when using paint stripper or working
with glass: most paint strippers are caustic
and glass can splinter when being removed.
Always wear safety goggles and rubber or
protective gloves.

NOTE

For metal-framed windows you need all
the equipment and materials listed except
for those marked '(wood)'. For wooden-
framed windows you need all the
equipment and materials listed except for
those marked '(metal)'.

Windows have been made in a
multitude of shapes and sizes and
many lend themselves to
conversion into stunning
ornamental mirrors. Removed
when frames have rotted or
houses are being 'updated',
sometimes an arched or
decoratively shaped window can
be found without difficulty at an
architectural reclamation yard,
awaiting transformation into a
beautiful mirror.

Before you start working on
any frame, give some thought to
how you will fix the mirror once
completed. Has it somewhere on
the reverse where picture wire can
be fitted? Does it have holes for
screw fixing? Could it be drilled to
accept screw eyes or is it
worthwhile getting fitting lugs
welded to the back? Every
window offers a different
challenge. If you intend using a
wooden frame, can the original
fittings be removed without
damaging the frame? It is
worthwhile thinking through the
project before you start. For this
project we have selected an
ancient cast-iron window saved
from a decommissioned church.
The window is irregular in shape
with no two panes the same size,
which adds to the appeal of the
mirror and justifies the little extra
effort needed to make it.

We have chosen to preserve
the aged and pitted appearance
of the cast iron on our project
mirror, but it could just as easily
be painted, gilded or given a
distressed finish to add to its
romantic appeal.

WINDOW MIRROR

METHOD

Note that alternative methods are given for wooden window frames. Read the instructions thoroughly before you begin to ensure that you use the correct method.

1 Clean the window frame with the stiff-bristled paintbrush then remove all the paint with the paint stripper, being careful to follow the manufacturer's instructions. Paint stripper is caustic so care should be taken. (We suggest using a paint-stripping service, which uses a hot caustic dip system and has the advantage of loosening any glass and putty still present in the frame.) Remove any glass, if you are using a frame with old glass, being careful not to break it, and put to one side. Clean off any residual paint and putty using a paint scraper and wire brush, paying particular attention to the glass rebate. (For wooden frames, use glasspaper instead of a wire brush.)

2 Make sure that the frame is dry and free of any dust or dirt. Apply clear furniture wax to the front of the frame with the small stiff brush, being careful not to get any wax into the glass rebate. Finish with some soft rag. (For wooden frames, wax both front and back, using an antique wax if preferred.) When the wax is dry, polish with the soft brush or soft cotton rag.

3 Carefully measure the glass rebate then mark and cut the mirror glass to the exact size. (If you are wary of cutting glass, a glazier will cut the glass to size for you.) Note that 2 mm ($\frac{1}{16}$ in) mirror glass is easier to cut than 4 mm ($\frac{3}{16}$ in) glass and is more suitable for smaller panes. (Because of the small panes in the window selected for this project, we have managed to use mirror glass cut from offcut and waste; we numbered each pane as it was cut to ensure a good fit when assembled.) Using the mastic gun, place a very small bead of mastic inside each frame rebate and fit the mirror glass, pressing it firmly into place. Apply the mastic carefully around the rear of the glass to secure it in place. Repeat until all the panes are filled. (For wooden frames, fill the glass rebate with softened putty and fit the glass in place. Use the glazing hammer and glazing pins to secure the glass. Fill the remaining rebate with putty and finish to a bevelled edge with the putty knife.)

Remove any excess mastic from the mirror surfaces and leave to set. Feed the heavy-duty picture wire through the lugs, screw eyes or plates on the back of the frame and tie in place. Use slip-proof knots and tighten with pliers, tying any excess wire to the lugs. Cast-iron frames are extremely heavy, so make sure that the wire used is sufficiently strong and that the knots used are slip-proof. Caution – when hanging the mirror, ensure that the fixings used will carry the weight of the mirror. Use rawlplugs and screws rather than picture hooks.

TRICK OF THE TRADE

Modern glass is produced by a 'float' process and is free of any blemishes or irregularities; old glass, on the other hand, is often full of imperfections, which can be part of its charm. If you prefer your mirror to have the appearance of antiquity, fit the new mirror glass behind refitted salvaged glass panes or glass cut from an old sheet. Ensure that the window rebate is sufficiently deep to take both sheets of glass and that the old glass and new mirror are clean before you fit them.

The next few pages show a
stunning array of shape and
form, all united by one thing in
common: illumination. Ideas from
glamorous, fragile-looking
chandeliers to lights made from a

LIGHT AND SHADE

humble roof tile are considered.
We take lighting for granted,
stretching out an arm to put on a
light switch, although even this
can now be done by remote
control. All it takes, however,
is an unexpected power cut to
throw us into panic and a frantic
search for matches and candles
– which usually turn up the
moment power is restored!

It seems strange to think that
less than fifty years ago many
houses, especially in rural areas,
had no electricity and that
people relied on paraffin lamps
and candles to do chores and
tasks as well as reading, sewing
and other leisure activities.
By contrast, today we have so
much choice in lighting:
unobtrusive low-voltage down-
lighters or washes of up-light to
accent interior details, and
dimmer switches that can swiftly
change the mood of a room.

ABOVE

Clear and some coloured plastic knives, forks and spoons have been used to create this eye-catching chandelier. An empty sunflower oil bottle covers the central hanging, while others have been cut down to make the candle cups. Fake candles have been made from the cardboard tubes found inside embroidery wools.

RIGHT

Chandelier by Madeleine Boulesteix, an artist working with a fantastic variety of salvaged materials including toast racks, Pyrex cups, glasses, plug chains and pastry cutters bought at charity shops and car-boot sales.

Lighting should complement the architecture of the area. If a modern chandelier is suspended within a sleek, contemporary interior, the two will blend and harmonise, yet an antique chandelier, sparkling and glowing, hung in the same interior becomes something the eye cannot resist, a dominant design feature and not in the least incongruous.

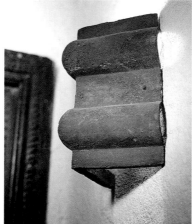

LEFT

A bulb has been placed under an iron pavement grill, radiating an arc of filtered light on to the wall above in the Bristol restaurant Byzantium.

BOTTOM LEFT

This double Roman terracotta roof tile has been secured to the wall to create an unusual, robust and practical rustic light fitting.

BOTTOM RIGHT

This pillar lamp was designed and made by cabinet maker Richard Wallace from thinly cut and painstakingly joined end grain softwood timber cut from pallets to give a soft, filtered light.

When searching out objects that could be given a new life as something quite different from their original use, we found that if no other idea sprang to mind, our discovery could always become yet another lamp or candle holder. The stainless-steel drum of a washing machine made a perfect hanging ceiling light fitting, and the gnarled oak blocks cut from sea defence posts became not only the legs of a glass-topped coffee table (see page 74) but also a most desirable table lamp base (see page 78). Another striking and much commented upon lamp base was made from a large glass carboy (see page 108), once used to transport glucose from France, and the rusty old metal hoops from an oak pickle barrel, attached to a chain found buried under a pile of discarded agricultural equipment, were transformed into a simple but eye-catching candlelit chandelier (see page 100).

In the chapter 'Wining and Dining', a heavy metal flower display stand bought at auction was recreated as a decorative candle stand (see page 22). Bed springs do not sound too promising, but surmounted with an orb-shaped candle, they can be transformed into a real talking point as a contemporary-looking centrepiece for the table (see page 122). Finally, wooden staircase newel posts, each drilled at one end for a giant candle, become imposing candle holders (see page 126).

HOOP CHANDELIER

EQUIPMENT

Wire brush
Palette knife
Glasspaper
Electric drill and selection of wood bits
Screwdriver
12 mm (½ in) paintbrush
Old toothbrush
Soft polishing brush
Soft cotton rag
Hacksaw

MATERIALS

Two barrel hoops of slightly different
    diameter
Scraps of waste wood
Two-part wood filler
Four mop- or broom-head holders
Eight 18 mm (¾ in) screws
Four 38 mm (1½ in) cup hooks
Four 38 mm (1½ in) screw eyes
Four steel marlin spikes
Four split rings
Four small lanyard hooks
Black satin finish stove paint
Black stove polish
Ceiling hook
Approximately 2.4 m (8 ft) metal chain
Candles

Safety notes

Lit candles are a potential fire hazard, so always
hang your chandelier sufficiently far enough from
the ceiling to ensure that there is no danger of fire
or smoke damage.
Rubber or protective gloves are recommended for
this project.
Make sure that all fittings are secure and that the
chandelier is fastened into a timber ceiling joist or
other structural timber. Under no circumstances
should it be fitted to laths, plaster or plasterboard.

Suspended from the ceiling, this simple but heavy metal design, which evolved from mainly industrial components, is in stark contrast to the delicate appearance of some of our other chandeliers.

As redundant oak whisky barrels or smaller pickle barrels used as garden planters finally give way to rot, remember to salvage the metal hoops. The cooper used these hoops of graduated sizes to secure the shaped wooden lathes in place, and to make this chandelier you will need to select two hoops of slightly different diameters. (Alternatively, you could use a wooden wheel for the frame, or, should you have access to welding equipment, a metal wheel.) You will also need some old-fashioned metal mop-head fixings to make candle holders and a number of heavy steel marlin spikes to dangle underneath. These weighty drops are not merely decorative but help to keep the chandelier both level, compensating for any differences in weight across the frame of the chandelier, and stable to prevent it swinging in inevitable draughts. They could be replaced with any other weighty item that could be attached to the screw eyes. The hoops came from our garden, the mop-head fittings were discovered in a reclamation yard and the steel marlin spikes were sold to us by a rope and sail maker; all the other fittings come from hardware shops. The sturdy chain, absolutely essential to take the weight of the finished chandelier, was part of a lot bought at a farm sale.

HOOP CHANDELIER

METHOD

1 Clean the barrel hoops with a wire brush to remove surface rust and grime. Place them on a work surface, one inside the other, and use scraps of wood to wedge the hoops apart so that a consistent gap is created between the hoops around their circumference. Fill the gap with two-part wood filler (any other plasticised filler that can be drilled and will hold a screw securely is an acceptable alternative) and smooth with the palette knife.

2 Turn the joined hoops over and fill the reverse of the gap with more filler. When the filler has cured, finish with glasspaper. Mark four equally spaced points on one surface of the filled and joined hoops and place a mop-head holder on each. Mark the fixing holes, remove the holders and drill holes to accept the 18 mm (¾ in) fixing screws. Attach the four mop-head holders with screws inserted into the filler.

3 Mark four points on the same side of the joined hoops midway between each fitted mop-head holder, then drill holes for and fit the four cup hooks. Turn the joined hoops over and drill four further holes, this time under the mop-head holders, and fit the screw eyes. (For added strength, the screw eyes and cup hooks can be screwed into the filler before it has fully cured; alternatively, coat their threads with filler before fitting them into the drilled holes.)

4 Paint the cup hooks, screw eyes and mop-head holders, together with the marlin spikes, split rings and lanyard hooks not yet fitted, with black satin finish stove paint and leave to dry. When they are fully dry, take the old toothbrush, dip it into the black stove polish and paint over the chandelier and fittings. When they are dry, polish to a light sheen with the soft brush and cotton rag.

5 Fix the ceiling hook securely to a roof joist or other structural timber above where your chandelier will hang; because of its weight, under no circumstances should it be fitted to laths, plaster or plasterboard. Decide on its height from the ceiling and cut the chain into two lengths, each double that measurement. Place the ends of each chain over opposing cup hooks and the centres on to the ceiling hook in order to hang the chandelier. Fit split rings and lanyard hooks to the marlin spikes and hang them from the screw eyes on the chandelier. Finally, insert candles in the mop-head holders and your chandelier is complete.

HIP TILE CEILING LIGHT

EQUIPMENT

Wire brush
Electric hammer drill
Masonry drill bit
Metal snips
Empty mastic gun
Dry sand or gravel
Metal or strong plastic bucket
Hacksaw
Pliers

MATERIALS

Three clay hip tiles
Waste lead sheet
Lead adhesive
Metal chain
Metal wire
Ceiling hook

SAFETY NOTE

This ceiling light is extremely heavy, so make sure
that all fittings are secure and that the ceiling hook
is fastened into a timber ceiling joist or other
structural timber. Under no circumstances should
it be fitted to laths, plaster or plasterboard.

We have always enjoyed the warmth and tradition of terracotta and search for different ways to use and enjoy this natural material.

Weathered roof tiles are particularly attractive, with lichens and water staining adding to their character. Hank Terry of Milo Design used reclaimed tiles as ceiling lights to great effect in the Bristol restaurant Byzantium and he offered to make a light from three hip tiles for this project. Hip tiles are used to cap the joint, or 'hip', of a roof, and innumerable patterns have been produced although all are of much the same general shape.

Terracotta roof tiles used as wall lights are quite a familiar sight in Spain and other Mediterranean countries, and we show you how to make one in the chapter 'Design and Detail' (see page 130).

You may choose to construct your ceiling light with the opening downwards rather than upwards, as ours is made, but whichever way round you choose, the light is heavy and must be hung on a chain fixed to a strong hook driven through the plaster and into a ceiling joist.

Other ideas we have seen for hanging lights are terracotta flower pots hung upside down and suspended from a ceiling, and particularly striking was a seaside villa in Italy where clear wine bottles, in groups of eight or ten, each with a light inside, provided the illumination. Architect Mark Watson has cleverly used a wooden grain hopper to make a shade for a centre light in the high-ceilinged sitting room in his holiday house, which was converted from a former corn mill.

HIP TILE CEILING LIGHT

METHOD

1 Select three hip tiles that are of equal size and relatively undamaged. Using the wire brush, clean off any lichen, dust or dirt from their surface, paying particular attention to the inside (or concave) surfaces. With the electric drill and masonry bit, drill a hole in the centre of the splayed end of each tile. Drill from the outside (or convex) side to prevent unsightly flaking of the clay surface where the drill bit emerges.

2 Cut the waste lead sheet with the metal snips into three strips each approximately 10 cm (4 in) wide and the length of the tiles. Place two tiles together, concave side up and supported by wooden blocks or spare tiles so that the edges fit tightly together and, using a mastic gun, apply a liberal quantity of lead adhesive to the full length of both tiles, approximately 50 mm (2 in) from both sides of the join. Press one cut lead strip on to the adhesive and press down to make a secure joint.

3 Place a quantity of dry sand or gravel into the bucket to support the tiles, then gently place the joined tiles into the bucket, pointed end down, and place the third tile in the bucket to make a tightly fitting cone shape of three tiles. It may prove necessary to add or remove sand or gravel to support the tiles properly in the bucket. When you are satisfied with the construction, apply lead adhesive approximately 50 mm (2 in) from both sides of the two remaining joins and secure with the lead strips. Make sure that the lead strips are securely bonded to the adhesive, then leave for at least twenty-four hours or until the adhesive has cured.

Remove the tiles from the bucket and clean off any residual adhesive. Measure three lengths of chain to slightly more than the height at which you wish to hang the finished light from the ceiling and cut to length with the hacksaw. Fit the chain lengths to the drilled holes in the tiles with metal wire and secure with the pliers. Use the pliers to make sure that the chain is securely fitted. Hang the finished light from the chains fitted to a hook driven into the ceiling.

CARBOY LAMP

EQUIPMENT

Electric drill
32 mm (1¼ in) tank cutting bit (to fit inside
    the bottle top)
Glasspaper
Multi-speed electrical tool and sanding
    head (optional)
18 mm (¾ in) auger or spade drill bit
Round wood file
Wood filler or two-part filling compound
    (optional)
Hammer
Glass cleaner
Lint-free cotton rag or absorbent kitchen
    paper
Electrician's screwdriver

MATERIALS

Piece of 50 mm (2 in) thick wood (preferably
    softwood)
Glass carboy bottle
Bottle lamp holder with side fitting and
    adjustable stem and lamp cord attached
Lamp holder
Lampshade
60 watt electric light bulb
Fused electric plug

METHOD

1 Use the 32 mm (1¼ in) tank cutting bit to cut a plug out of the piece of 50 mm (2 in) thick timber. You will have to measure the diameter of the inside of the top of the bottle you are using and cut a plug slightly larger than that measurement. Use glasspaper or the multi-speed electrical tool and sanding head to sand the plug down to a lightly tapered shape until it will fit tightly inside the top of the bottle.

2 Use the electric drill and auger or spade bit, placed in the hole already cut in the centre of the plug, to cut a second hole, 18 mm (¾ in) in diameter, in the plug. Again, this measurement depends on the bottle lamp holder you are using. Most are made from plastic and the stem is designed to compress to fit differing hole sizes, so adjust the size of your hole to fit. If necessary, enlarge this hole to fit the lamp holder stem with the round wood file or multi-speed electrical tool and sanding head.

3 Gently insert the stem of the lamp holder inside the plug so that it is securely held. If the lamp holder is loose, you can use wood filler or two-part filling compound to fix it in place.

Clean the inside of the bottle, because once the lamp holder is inserted you will not be able to clean it. A simple way to remove staining from the inside of a glass container is to fill it with a small amount of sharp gravel and shake vigorously. Rinse with hot soapy water and leave to drain.

4 Carefully place the wooden plug and lamp holder into the top of the bottle; it should be a tight fit. Tap the plug home into the bottle using a hammer cushioned with a scrap of timber, gently working around the circumference of the plug. If the plug is too tight a fit, there is a danger that you may break the bottle as the plug is driven home, so err on the side of caution, remove the plug and lamp holder, sand off a little more wood and try again until the plug sits securely inside the neck of the bottle.

Clean the outside of the bottle with glass cleaner and polish with cotton rag or absorbent kitchen paper. Unscrew the top of the lamp holder and fit the shade holder and your chosen lampshade. Insert the light bulb and attach the fused electric plug to the lamp cord fitted to the lamp holder.

Safety note

Electricity can be dangerous; if you are in any doubt, we advise that all electrical fittings are checked by a qualified electrician. If a metal lamp holder is used, it is vital that three-core wire is used and that the earth is connected to both the lamp holder and the electric plug.

Hand-blown glass has an enduring appeal. It is strong and fluid yet fragile and delicate, with light dancing off to reflect its shape and the colours of the room around. The carboy we selected as a lamp base is a utilitarian clear glass bottle that was originally designed to transport large quantities of glucose from France for use in the English wine-making trade, protected by a wooden cradle in transit. Since glass resists corrosion, carboys were also used to transport acid, but these bottles have now been replaced by plastic to ensure that the contents last the journey. No two carboys are identical, differing slightly in the overall shape, the bubbles embedded in the glass and in colour – they can sometimes be found in a glorious green hue.

Some of the bottles filled with brightly coloured liquids that at one time were seen in every chemist's window would, if one could buy them, convert into superb lamps and, since fashion is cyclical, we may again see Chianti bottles in their woven grass cradles converted into lamps, just as they once were seen in every self-respecting bistro throughout the 1960s.

GLOBE LIGHT

EQUIPMENT

Electric drill
12 mm (½ in) auger or spade drill bit
Tenon saw
High-speed multi-purpose tool with saw
    attachment (optional)
12 mm (½ in) wood chisel
Lint-free cotton rag
Electrician's screwdriver

MATERIALS

Wooden tent pole base plate (or similar
    wooden round)
Medium brown furniture wax
18 mm (¾ in) screws
Brown frame sealant
Green baize or felt
Rubberised glue
Glass globe

ELECTRICAL

Approx. 2 m (2 yd) two-core electrical amp
    flex (or three-core if a metal lamp fitting
    is used)
Metal or plastic flat-based lamp holder
Fused electric plug
Electric light bulb (60 watt maximum)

METHOD

1 Take the tent pole base plate and drill through the centre from the top with the 12 mm (½ in) auger or spade bit. It is advisable to place the base plate on a piece of waste wood, unless your work surface will not mind the drill bit passing into it. (If you are using a wooden round with no indented area, you must drill or cut a rebate in the top sufficient to house the globe glass light comfortably.)

2 Turn the wooden base over so that the bottom faces upwards and, with a tenon saw, make two cuts approximately 12 mm (½ in) apart and 12 mm (½ in) deep leading from the drilled centre hole to the outside edge. (A high-speed multi-purpose tool with saw attachment will make very short work of this job.) Use the 12 mm (½ in) wood chisel to remove the wood between the saw cuts to leave a groove for the electric lamp flex.

3 Apply a liberal application of medium brown furniture wax to the top and sides of the base, rubbing it well into the wood with clean, lint-free cotton rag. Make sure not to get any wax on the bottom surface of the base. Leave the wax to dry and be absorbed into the wood, then polish with some more clean rag. A second application of wax will improve the finish.

4 Pass the electric lamp flex up through the centre of the wooden base and, with the electrician's screwdriver, fit it to the flat-based lamp holder. Screw the lamp holder to the bottom of the rebate in the base with the 18 mm (¾ in) screws. Fit the electric plug to the other end, pull the flex taught and secure into the groove cut in the bottom of the base with brown frame sealant. Leave the sealant to cure.

When the sealant has cured, cut the baize or felt to the shape of the bottom of the lamp base and fit in place with rubberised glue. When the glue has dried, insert an electric light bulb into the lamp holder and place the glass globe light over the top.

Safety note

Electricity can be dangerous; if you are in any doubt, we advise that all electrical fittings are checked by a qualified electrician. If a metal lamp holder is used, it is vital that three-core wire is used and that the earth wire is connected to both the lamp holder and the electric plug.

To make this simple but effective light, with its soft, unobtrusive glow, you need only three main components: a base, a shade and the electrical fittings.

In our constant search for salvaged materials, we often turn to the detritus-filled premises of our friendly government surplus supplier. We knew from experience that after a couple of hours in his premises we would leave full of inspiration and, fortunately for him, several purchases. Clambering into the back of a malodorous old container body used as storage in the yard we hit upon rows of wooden rounds, which resembled truckles of farmhouse cheeses lined up in a dairy.

We were unable to guess their origins, but Lawrence enlightened us: they were the turned ash or beech pole base plates used to stop the poles of old marquees sinking into soft ground. After many years of service, the canvas marquees became redundant. They were then either passed on to the Boy Scouts or donated to charities, who send them out as emergency relief shelters to disaster areas worldwide (minus their wooden feet). Marquees in too poor a state of repair for use were burnt or thrown away, and all that was left behind were the tent poles, pole bases and guy rope pegs we discovered on our visit.

The spherical glass, opalescent, clear or sometimes patterned, can be found in different sizes from architectural reclamation yards. We found ours at Au Temps Perdu, where owner John Chapman, an enthusiast and mine of information, told us that they were the enclosed covers for bathroom lights.

COLUMN LAMP

The column lamp we have featured here was designed by John Edmonds. The vertical beam of light thrown by the hole in the top of the column and the muted illumination shining through the wooden beading and tissue paper used in its construction give this light an Eastern feel.

John has designed a number of lamps using everything from lead, old terracotta land drains rescued after almost two hundred years underground, figured and ancient oak and elm, and even glass salvaged from the cockpit of a dismantled aircraft. He has been working with recycled materials for thirty years and now employs over twenty designers and craftsmen working in timber, stone, metal and glass, interpreting his designs, making and restoring furniture and undertaking a variety of design, construction and restoration projects throughout Britain and abroad.

The column lamp can be made in various sizes, from hardwood, softwood or any number of different materials. For this project we have selected timber cut from old softwood joists for the base and column construction and salvaged beading for the connecting structure. Redundant brass stair rods also make unusual connectors.

EQUIPMENT

Electric planer or hand plane
Try square
Sash clamps
Medium-grade glasspaper
Sanding block
Tape measure
Compass made from string, pencil and drawing pin
Jigsaw and fine wood-cutting blade
Electric drill
12 mm (½ in) spade drill bit
Straight edge
Handsaw
Soft cotton rag
Hammer
12 mm (½ in) wood chisel or craft knife
Waxing brush or stiff-bristled paintbrush
Paste brush
Electrician's screwdriver

MATERIALS

The project lamp has been designed as a table lamp but all dimensions are approximate and can be adjusted for the materials available and the size of the lamp you are making, which may be scaled up or down.

Approx. 2 m (2 yd) of 20 cm x 50 mm (8 x 2 in) salvaged softwood joists
Wood glue
Furniture wax polish
Approx. 9 m (9 yd) of 18 x 10 mm (¾ x ⅜ in) planed quadrant, cut into twelve 75 cm (30 in) lengths
Tissue or other translucent paper (handmade paper is an alternative)
Wallpaper paste

ELECTRICAL

Fused electric plug
Two-core lamp flex (or three-core if a metal lamp fitting is used)
Plastic batten lamp holder
Electric light bulb (60 watt maximum)

Safety note

Electricity can be dangerous; if you are in any doubt, we advise that all electrical fittings are checked by a qualified electrician. If metal lamp fittings are used, it is vital that three-core wire is used and that the earth wire is connected to both the lamp holder and the electric plug.

COLUMN LAMP

METHOD

1 Cut the 20 cm x 5 mm (8 x 2 in) softwood joists into four 30 cm (12 in) lengths and two 38 cm (15 in) lengths. Plane one edge of each cut length, making sure that it is square with the try square. Take two pieces of each cut length and, using glue and sash clamps, join them together planed edge to planed edge. Repeat with the remaining lengths until you have two pieces of timber 40 x 30 cm (16 x 12 in) and one 40 x 38 cm (16 x 15 in). Leave for at least twenty-four hours to dry before removing the sash clamps. When the glue is dry, plane the faces of the timber and use the glasspaper and sanding block to finish.

Mark a point at the centre of face of the 38 cm (15 in) joined length. Take a length of string and tie one end to a drawing pin placed firmly on the centre mark and tie a pencil to the other end of the string, 18 cm (7 in) from the centre, to make a simple compass. Holding the centre pin in one hand and the pencil in the other, draw a 36 cm (14 in) circle on the board to create the outline of the lamp base; put to one side. Shorten the string to 14 cm (5½ in) and draw circles 28 cm (11 in) in diameter on both 30 cm (12 in) joined lengths to create outlines for the column base and top. Shorten the string to 75 mm (3 in) and, using the same centre points, draw two further circles, 15 cm (6 in) in diameter, inside the 28 cm (11 in) drawn circles.

2 Using the jigsaw, cut carefully round the rings to make three circular boards, one 36 cm (14 in) and two 28 cm (11 in) in diameter. Cut 12 mm (½ in) holes in the centres of all three boards with the electric drill and spade bit. Take the 36 cm (14 in) board (lamp base) and, on the underside starting at the drilled centre hole, draw two lines 12 mm (½ in) apart with a pencil to the outside edge. Use the handsaw to cut along the pencil lines to a depth of approximately 10 mm (⅜ in), then remove the waste wood with the wood chisel to create a channel for the lamp flex. Cut out 15 cm (6 in) centres in the 28 cm (11 in) column base and top, using the drilled hole for jigsaw blade access. Smooth the exposed sawn edges with glasspaper.

3 Depending on the final appearance desired, wax and polish the column base and top and lamp base with the soft rag to the desired finish. Take the column base and top and, with the drill and spade bit, cut twelve equally spaced holes around the outside of both boards approximately 18 mm (¾ in) from the outside edge and approximately 12 mm (½ in) deep. Ensure that the twelve 75 cm (30 in) lengths of quadrant beading are free from knots or bends and trim the ends with a chisel or craft knife to fit tightly into 12 mm (½ in) holes. Drive the twelve sections of beading into the drilled holes to join the column base and top, and secure with wood glue. Leave to dry.

4 Take a number of approximately 1 m (1 yd) torn lengths of your selected paper, paste one side with wallpaper paste, then carefully stretch them round the lamp over the beading. When the beading is covered to your satisfaction (several layers may be required), leave the paper to dry. You have now completed the construction of your lamp.

Fit the fused plug to one end of the electric lamp flex. Feed the other end of the flex from the underside of the lamp base through the drilled hole and fit it to the plastic batten lamp holder, screwed to the top of the base over the hole. Place the light bulb in the lamp holder then place the assembled column over the top.

In this chapter we illustrate a number of designs that are firstly functional but must work visually too. It is worth remembering that even when a design has been specially commissioned, it can

Where companies or individuals have conscientiously striven to salvage and reuse materials, the end results can be superb. Handmade clay bricks have a wonderful depth of colour,

DESIGN AND DETAIL

be quite a challenge to make it work in a practical sense, and when the item or product is old and has been made for another entirely different use or situation, the challenge is that much greater. Of course, the easy way out is to buy 'off the shelf', rather than consider how something might be adapted for reuse, but finding a solution is half the fun!

and even the heavy bricks rescued from the inside of outdated night store heaters, which usually end their days as hard core, make stunning floors. Roof slates, laid on concrete, their nail holes filled with lead and polished to a gleam, can be transfigured into a floor of great beauty that seems to stretch to infinity.

TOP 1

Solid mahogany doors, rescued from a redundant bank, divide the entrance hall in this house from a more formal inner hall. The gold leaf lettering is original.

TOP 2

Wooden staircase spindles have been cut down the middle lengthways to provide a decorative detail for the shelves of a well-proportioned but plain bookcase at Charlton House Hotel.

TOP 3

Milo Design have used roof slates salvaged from a church to cover a large floor area in the Bristol restaurant Byzantium.

TOP 4

Once installed in an ancient manor house, this floor was taken up at some stage and subsequently found piled into buckets in a reclamation yard. Although badly damaged, it was reassembled and relaid, with any missing sections cleverly matched up.

TOP 5

This well-worn but delicately patterned early encaustic terracotta floor once belonged in a historic and rather grand Jacobean house.

TOP 6

This oak staircase was designed by architect Mark Watson for a converted stable block, with a curved oak stall partition forming the handrail. The iron supports and elm boards on the wall behind were reclaimed from the original building.

RIGHT

This balcony was built in the converted barn adjoining designer John Edmonds' farmhouse to divide a bedroom from the seating area below. The supports were made from driftwood, dried and air blasted with crushed walnut shells, and the rail and base from aged oak faced with spalted (diseased) elm.

Wood for floors is probably the most commonly reclaimed and reused material. Medieval oak cut from French farm buildings, pitch pine planks cut from a Victorian mill, a parquet floor in some exotic hardwood rescued from a modest office building, or yellow pine from a redundant factory all cry out for rescue and sympathetic treatment. Most striking of all was an interlocking gymnasium floor taken up, its original markings preserved and relaid in an apparently random pattern – seemingly simple but a time-consuming task. Where time and money are involved, it is easy to see why so many good-quality materials are dumped or destroyed by contractors anxious to complete their work within a deadline.

It's all in the detail. Detail is the molten lead that filled the nail holes in a slated floor or the simplicity of a moulded block of wood used to hold open a door; the care the craftsman takes to carve the finest shape; the incongruous choice of colour in a casually placed object. All those things that

accentuate, add interest and make a room complete make such an important contribution to the overall design.

Ornamental and decorative detail is shown in the unknown origins of the textured leather moulding in the entrance hall or the split wooden staircase spindle, which added another dimension to an otherwise ordinary bookcase at Charlton House Hotel; the gold leaf lettering on a mahogany door in a Wiltshire house and the distinctive walnut shell blasted driftwood balcony in John Edmonds' home. All have a beauty, fascinating, functionless but exquisite in their shapes and hues.

Not all detail needs be purely decorative. An original, basic but functional wooden lock on a sixteenth-century oak door, and plain metal rods that perfectly complement a reclaimed oak staircase rescued from the same building are practical features but at the same time they help to break up a line and relieve the eye from too much timber – pure and simple, and yet precise.

SPINDLE BOOKCASE

EQUIPMENT

Pliers
Bench saw or band saw
Tenon saw
Hammer
18 mm (¾ in) wood chisel
Craft knife (optional)
Glasspaper
Electric drill
Drill bit to fit 75 mm (3 in) screws
Screwdriver
Waxing brush or stiff-bristled paintbrush
Soft lint-free cotton rag
Soft polishing brush

MATERIALS

Several stair spindles
Old bookcase
45 mm (1¾ in) panel pins
Wood glue
Four bun feet
Four 75 mm (3 in) screws
Antique brown furniture wax

METHOD

1 Before commencing the construction of this bookcase, the spindles must be split in half along their length. It is perfectly possible, if extremely time-consuming, to do this with a handsaw, but a much better result can be achieved if the spindles are cut with a bench or band saw. Remember before you start cutting to remove any nails that may still be present in the spindles; failure to do this may result in serious damage to the machinery and, more importantly, may cause the spindle being cut to 'snatch', resulting in injury to the machine operator.

2 Lay the bookcase on its back on a work surface, select two half-spindles for the sides of the bookcase, trim them to size with the tenon saw and secure temporarily in place with panel pins. For the shelves, we have used spindles cut so that two opposing pieces cut from the one spindle make a balanced pattern on each shelf. Should you wish to achieve a more idiosyncratic appearance, use one whole cut spindle for each shelf front. Shape the ends where they butt against the spindles attached to the bookcase sides with a chisel or craft knife and glasspaper to make a tight fit. Secure temporarily with panel pins.

3 Remove all the temporarily fitted spindles, apply wood glue to them and replace with the panel pins driven well home. If your bookcase is not fitted with feet, the spindle fitted to the bottom shelf may prevent it standing properly. It is simple to add feet to raise it slightly off the floor to eliminate this problem. We have used softwood bun feet made from cut-down old tent pole finials. Drill though each foot from the underside, apply wood glue and secure to the bottom corners of the bookcase with 75 mm (3 in) screws.

4 Put the bookcase on one side to allow the glue to dry thoroughly. When it is dry, apply antique brown furniture wax with a waxing brush or stiff-bristled paintbrush, paying particular attention to ensuring that the wax is brushed into the corners and the spindle mouldings. Rub the wax well into the wood with the soft cotton rag, and leave to dry. Polish with the soft polishing brush and finish with clean cotton rag. A greater density of colour can be achieved with a second application of wax, and the finish can be maintained by occasional polishing with a soft cloth.

Safety note

If you are using any power-cutting equipment, particularly a bench or band saw, eye protection should be used.
We advise that protective gloves are used for this project.

Spindles are the turned supports for the banister rail on a staircase. Made in many different lengths, they were made in their millions when wood-turning machinery was introduced. They are easy to find and here we suggest some uses for them. Matching or not, barley twist or plain, spindles split in half make a decorative and inexpensive moulding perfectly suited to enhance a modest shelf unit to give it a presence it might otherwise not have. Split spindles can adorn all sorts of other furniture, from kitchen cupboards and bathroom units to wooden mirrors, and in this chapter we also show you how to turn one into an elegant candlestick.

You could undertake this project leaving both the bookcase and spindles in their original painted state. However, if you wish to do this, all paintwork should be cleaned with sugar soap, rubbed down with glasspaper and undercoated before being repainted. Old bookcases and spindles often have several layers of paint, and the thickness of these coats can obscure some of the finer and more attractive detail. We recommend that to achieve the best results the bookcase and spindles should be stripped.

Stripping can be undertaken using a commercially available paint stripper, but this is a laborious and unpleasant job that requires protective gloves and clothing. Much more simple is to have your bookcase and spindles stripped by one of the numerous professional stripping services, which use a hot caustic bath to achieve an excellent result.

BED SPRING CANDLE HOLDERS

EQUIPMENT

Fine-grade wire wool
Metal polish
Soft cotton rag

MATERIALS

Bed spring
Metal lacquer spray
Globe-shaped candle

METHOD

1 Gently remove any corrosion with the wire wool, taking care not to rub off the copper plating. Apply the metal polish with a soft cotton rag and burnish with a clean rag. Spray with metal lacquer to preserve the finish and prevent subsequent tarnishing. Place a globe-shaped candle in the top of each spring.

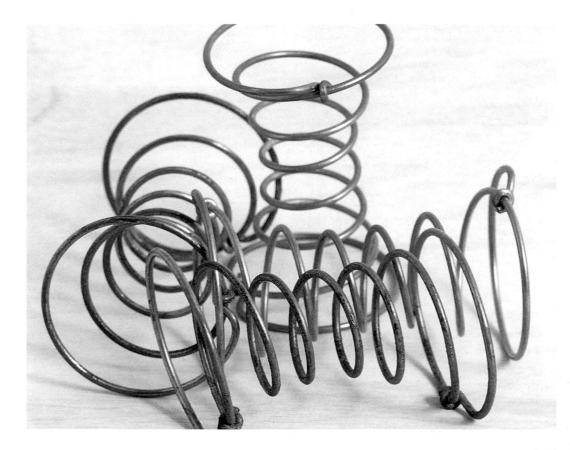

They may compare unfavourably to a pair of solid silver candlesticks passed down through the family over several generations, but our bed spring candle holders are certain to become a talking point, if not a conversation stopper. They illustrate the point that the most unlikely objects can be turned into something desirable and these coiled candle holders are both unusual and, more importantly, fun. Like many people, we have collected candlesticks in many different sizes and materials, from ceramics, glass and metal to a set of five we designed and had turned by a local craftsman from fallen, diseased sycamore, graduating in size from over 1.5 m to less than 30 cm (12 in) in height.

We have candles in Victorian ink bottles, night lights in dimpled glasses found at car boot sales, and others in small terracotta flower pots that we have covered with gilt and silver leaf to make a festive table display, particularly at Christmas. As long as the candle fits safely into its receptacle and does not overbalance, there is no limit to the number of objects that can be adapted to become candle holders. Flickering candlelight can illuminate every room of your home!

Scrap yards and car-breakers are good hunting grounds, and at one we managed to salvage a number of copper-plated steel bed or chair springs with the plating still intact. The coiled, almost sculptural shape of these springs, surmounted by globe-shaped candles, suggests that they may have been commissioned by a master metal-smith.

WOOD BLOCK TABLE

EQUIPMENT

Tape measure
Large set square
Chalk or felt-tip pen
Chain saw
Sanding flap disc
Angle grinder
Fibre sanding disc

MATERIALS

Large wooden block or post

METHOD

1 Measure the block and calculate how it can be cut into two equal parts, both having ends that are square. Translate these measurements on to the wooden block using the set square and chalk or felt-tip pen. Prop the block on scrap wood so that is raised off the ground and, being careful to follow the chalk or ink marks, cut off one end square with the chain saw. Continue with the chain saw until you have two equally sized blocks and are satisfied that the ends are square.

2 Fit the sanding flap disc to the angle grinder and remove any rough, discoloured or damaged timber from the sides and one end; work slowly along the length of the block to minimise unsightly sanding marks. Finish to a smooth surface with the angle grinder and fibre sanding disc.

The finished blocks, complete with the evidence of chain sawing on their exposed tops, make extremely effective occasional or lamp tables, perfect for a minimalist interior.

Safety note

Chain saws are potentially extremely dangerous. If you are unfamiliar with their use, seek professional help.
In any event, always use a powerbreaker plug and wear full protective clothing and eye protection when using a chain saw. Eye protection and a dust mask should also be used when sanding with an angle grinder.

Unlikely as it may seem, these unusually large chunks of timber, which weigh enough to make you regret not weight training before you move them, once supported the metal crash barriers between opposing lanes on a motorway. Now that they are slowly being replaced by purpose-made metal supports, we were able to acquire enough for our needs.

Not wishing to compromise the masculine shape and powerful form of the supports, we felt that the best option was to make them slightly more manageable by cutting them in half to make two smaller cubes. With the warmth of the honey gold wood, they are beautiful in their simplicity, works of art, set off with a ceramic pot and placed either side of our Railway Bed (see page 40).

Should you have difficulty in locating a similar motorway barrier block, any large wooden block will serve just as well, and the project is ideally suited to an old tree trunk or bole, squared off to size.

SPINDLE CANDLESTICK

This elegant candlestick was made from a turned wooden spindle. Found in differing lengths and designs in most reclamation yards, spindles are commonly made of softwood, although as many were made from species of wood no longer harvested, some can be quite hard.

Because so many spindles were made but there are not all that many uses for them, many yards end up burning them for firewood. Spindles are very often varnished or painted when acquired but can be professionally stripped in a bath of hot caustic soda or stripped by hand with commercial paint stripper, as we did to the spindle used for this project. Time-consuming and unpleasant though it is, the result is well worth the effort and we achieved the bleached, aged effect we sought.

Stripped spindles can be waxed and polished, or left unstripped and repainted if preferred, although they should be rubbed down and undercoated before a new coat of paint is applied. We chose to leave the spindle unpolished and selected the 18 cm (7 in) square piece of 25 mm (1 in) softwood plank to match it for colour and texture. Whichever way you treat your spindle, there is great pleasure to be derived from the soft, warm glow of candlelight. You may choose to make any length of candlestick from old spindles, the size being dependent only on the length of the spindle used. Some spindle patterns have square mouldings along their length and these can be used to create shorter candlesticks.

EQUIPMENT

Hammer
Glasspaper
Tape measure
Electric drill
25 mm (1 in) spade drill bit
Pliers
Tenon saw
Set square
38 mm (1½ in) wood chisel
Craft knife
Sash or G clamp

MATERIALS

18 cm (7 in) square of 12 mm (½ in) thick
    plywood or medium density fibreboard
    (MDF)
18 cm (7 in) square of 25 mm (1 in) thick
    softwood plank
Wood glue
32 mm (1¼ in) panel pins
Stair spindle

SPINDLE CANDLESTICK

METHOD

1 Join the squares of plywood and softwood together with wood glue and hammer together with 32 mm (1¼ in) panel pins. Plywood or MDF glued to the softwood will prevent it distorting and ensure that the candlestick has a flat base for stability. Use the glasspaper to smooth off the sawn edges.

2 When the glue has dried, mark the centre of the softwood square, place the base on a piece of waste timber and, with the electric drill and 25 mm (1 in) spade bit, drill a hole though both the softwood and the plywood underneath. For a neat finish, drill until the tip of the bit emerges, then turn over and complete the hole, drilling from the plywood side.

3 Take the spindle, use the pliers to remove any nails, then trim both ends square with the tenon saw. Select which end of the spindle is to be the top and which is to be inserted into the base. (This will usually be evident: the end with the shorter section of square moulding will form the top.) Sand off the sawn edges on the top end.

4 Draw a line with a pencil and the set square round the bottom of the spindle 38 mm (1½ in) from the end. Use the tenon saw to make a cut on each face to leave about 25 mm (1 in) uncut wood at the centre. Prise off the cut wood with the wood chisel to leave a core of approximately 25 mm (1 in) in the end. Trim to the exact measurement with the craft knife and glasspaper.

5 Turn the spindle round so that you are able to work on the top and clamp it to the work surface with a sash or G clamp to hold it securely in place. Mark the centre at the top of the end of the spindle with a pencil and carefully drill a hole approximately 18 mm (¾ in) deep with the electric drill and spade bit.

6 Apply wood glue to the trimmed 25 mm (1 in) end of the spindle and insert it into the previously drilled 25 mm (1 in) hole made in the base. Trim off any wood that protrudes below the bottom of the base, ensure that the inserted spindle is vertical, then wipe off any residual wood glue and leave to set.

HIP TILE WALL LIGHT

EQUIPMENT

Wire brush
Battery-powered electric drill
Masonry drill bit
Electrician's screwdriver

MATERIALS

Clay roof hip tile
Angled batten lamp holder
Five rawlplugs
Two 38 mm (1½ in) screws
Electric light bulb (60 watt maximum)
Three 65 mm (2½ in) screws

METHOD

1 Select a hip tile with a curve such that when placed on a flat surface it is sufficiently deep to house the angled batten lamp holder and electric light bulb easily. Place it on the work surface and remove any residual cement, lichen or unsightly staining with the wire brush. With the concave side down, drill three holes with the electric drill and masonry bit, one at the centre of the apex and one at each of the bottom corners. It is a good idea to drill through the tile into a piece of scrap timber; drill carefully and try to prevent the tile being damaged by the emerging drill bit. When the tile is drilled, put it to one side.

2 Make sure that the power is turned off at the mains. Hold the angled batten lamp holder over the wires emerging from the wall in the location you wish to fix it, mark the screw holes with a pencil and put it to one side. Use the battery-operated electric drill and masonry bit to drill holes to a depth of approximately 38 mm (1½ in) at the points marked with a pencil; insert a rawlplug in each. Be careful not to drill into concealed wires. Fit the wires emerging from the wall securely to the reverse of the angled batten

lamp holder, then fix the lamp holder itself to the wall with the 38 mm (1½ in) screws driven into the rawlplugs.

3 Fit the light bulb to the lamp holder and place the hip tile carefully over it in the position desired. For a down-lighter, the opening should face down; for an up-lighter, the opening should face up. Mark the holes drilled in the tile with a pencil and put it to one side. Drill holes at least 50 mm (2 in) deep at the three marked points, being very careful not to drill through concealed electric wires, and insert the rawlplugs. Replace the hip tile in position and secure to the wall using the 65 mm (2½ in) screws driven into the rawlplugs.

Clay hip tiles are extremely heavy, so make sure that the finished light is securely fitted to the wall and that fixings are sufficiently strong to take the weight. For safety, make sure that the light bulb does not touch either the wall or the rear of the tile. When you are satisfied with the appearance of your wall light, switch on the power.

Safety note

Electricity is dangerous; we advise that a properly qualified and experienced electrician is consulted before any electrical work is undertaken. Always turn off the electricity at the mains before starting any work. When drilling close to a fitted wall light, be very careful not to damage buried wires.

A good investment is a wire detector, which can be used to locate hidden electrical cables, thus minimising the danger of damaging wiring when drilling.

 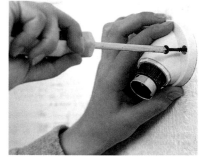 

Wall lights can add a quality of light and ambience to a room quite impossible to achieve with ceiling lights, however decorative they are. The variety of wall lights that can be bought from interior design and lighting shops is extensive, but many salvaged materials can be used to make quite singular and attractive alternatives.

Old car headlamps can be adapted to serve as effective wall lights, just as other car parts, including the hubcaps fitted to wire holders, can be converted into stunning shaded wall lights. The everyday metal kitchen colander cries out to be a wall light; in fact, there is no reason why you should not be able to make a wall light out of almost anything that takes your fancy.

We have selected hip tiles for this project because they are readily found, inexpensive to buy and come in numerous different shapes, patterns and sizes. Hank and Sophia Terry of Milo Design have used a number of different hip, ridge and roofing tiles in numerous innovative interiors, and examples of some of these are illustrated elsewhere in this book.

Finally, hip tiles can be used as both up-lighters, with the opening at the top, or turned over, as we demonstrate in this project, to act as down-lighters to illuminate a painting or a piece of furniture, or to provide muted atmospheric and unusual lighting.

We are all slowly becoming more environmentally aware, religiously recycling our empty bottles and old newspapers, but in reality

fittings are in considerable demand and many a reclamation dealer would jump for joy at the prospect of handling the

HOW TO GET IT, HOW TO DO IT

most of us merely pay lip service to recycling and conservation.

Currently less than 5 per cent of all re-usable materials are recycled and perhaps the most striking example is in the building industry. Demolition contractors know that much of what they destroy has a commercial value. Old bricks are greatly sought after, but generally end up as hard core; structural timbers, the life-blood of many reclaimed furniture makers, are so often used as firewood; cast iron radiators and ceramic bathroom

hardwood parquet floors which are ripped up and taken to landfill sites.

Contractors and developers know that the return they could achieve for these materials is outweighed by the time it would take to separate and find an outlet for them. Even scrap metal, of which there is such a large amount in any building, no longer fetches the price it once did and ends up discarded, further increasing the pressure on already hard-pressed and expensive landfill sites.

TOP LEFT

Sought-after cast iron radiators, crates of stone, an old cider millstone and a redundant Victorian timber-framed fishing lodge await buyers at Wells Reclamation.

TOP CENTRE

A pile of old triple Roman roof tiles and a number of increasingly rare glass tiles wait to be used on the roof of an extension to an old farmhouse.

TOP RIGHT

A stack of fine terracotta pipes and drains discovered during recent land drainage work await conversion into lamps at John Edmonds' workshop.

BOTTOM

Interesting shapes of 'green' oak offcuts from massive roof beams made for an ancient beamed ceiling undergoing repair.

Fortunately there is a growing awareness of the problem and an increase in the small number of people trying to do something about what we are losing. The decision to use old materials should not be driven by conscience alone. Salvaged items were often made with materials and a commitment to craftsmanship that is sadly lacking in their modern counterparts, and some would argue they are often far more beautiful. A wrought-iron support bracket recently seen at Au Temps Perdu, reclamation guru Pete Chapman's yard in Bristol, was a fine example of a Victorian craftsman adding time-consuming embellishments to a part of the structure which was only revealed when the bracket was removed from its site.

Softwoods used for utilitarian objects in past years are often from species which are no longer harvested or were cut from timber of a size not found in today's commercially forested plantation trees. The grain, texture and colour of many reclaimed timbers are almost impossible to find in modern woods; old handmade bricks can never be replicated and the patina, shape and coloration of stone and slate which has been worn by the feet of generations is difficult to emulate.

Whilst it is no longer true that all reclaimed materials are less expensive than the modern alternatives, inexpensive raw materials for re-use or conversion into new and different purposes are all around us. Builders' skips are an obvious source of useful items, farm sales are well worth attending, junk and charity shops can offer exciting finds and even salvaged metal merchants will sell items for their scrap value. Government surplus dealers deserve a mention, especially Lawrence Harper of Harper's Bazaar in Worcestershire who has shared much of his knowledge and imbued us with enthusiasm for the re-use of his well-made and robust utilitarian stock.

Reclamation yards are the place to find a vast resource of architectural antiques, reclaimed and salvaged materials all under one roof and their number has proliferated over recent years. Some years ago enthusiasts Thornton Kay and Hazel Matravers established SALVO, the organisation which is today recognised as being the hallmark of the reliable dealer. SALVO has a worldwide membership committed to the observance of its voluntary code, which is designed to promote ethical reclamation and prevent the trade in stolen artifacts or items removed from listed buildings.

SALVO publishes a regular newsletter and details of dealers in architectural antiques, reclaimed materials and antique garden ornaments as well as demolition companies, architects, craftsmen and numerous other professionals, listed by county or country, together with many other useful addresses. Their website (www.salvo.co.uk) includes the home pages of a number of their subscribers and is well worth visiting.

The web is an expanding source of information and, increasingly, reclaimed materials. A number of local authorities and US State bodies run regularly updated web information on people and organisations both selling and looking for salvaged items. The Old House Web (www.theoldhouseweb.com) is a worthwhile site for restoration enthusiasts and offers a free email newsletter to subscribers, including useful information and contacts to would-be house renovators, albeit with an American bias.

Travel abroad stimulates inspiration for designs and new uses for reclaimed materials. It also presents a chance to rescue materials that you may be lucky enough to come across. A visit to Catalonia resulted in a return flight carrying ancient olive jars (some with the residual oil still in them) as hand luggage. We were able to use them very successfully as decorative features in the garden. While driving through France we found some ancient encaustic tiles tipped in a pile at the edge of a wood where we had stopped for a picnic. On the return trip from a visit to clients in the Netherlands we rather fortuitously discovered a skip in Antwerp and were able to fill our van with fine handmade bricks discarded from a period property, which we later used to make a beautiful floor.

Eastern Europe is today being ravaged by foreign dealers hungry for antique furniture and decorative architectural antiques whilst India and the Far East, where the scant and poorly policed conservation laws go largely ignored, are next on the list for rapacious exploitation.

France remains a rich source of under-appreciated salvage, much of which is still disregarded. Emmaüs, a charity established to provide shelter for the homeless, has long been a rich resource of reclaimed materials. Once the recipients of cast-off clothing and no longer needed furniture sold to fund their work, today it is a highly professional organisation, represented in most major French centres, where a vast resource of artifacts and salvage is collected for sale to the increasing number of trade and private purchasers who beat a trail to its doors. Emmaüs, Matériaux Anciens, Dépôts Vente and Demolitions are all rich sources of salvage throughout France.

Wherever you locate your salvaged materials, whether searching for a particular piece or discovering something 'just too good to miss', use your imagination, do a bit of lateral thinking when looking for alternative approaches for their use and treat them with respect. However modest they may be, they have a history and perhaps as well as owning something which is unique, you will have made some small dent in the blanket of apathy which surrounds all things considered past their 'useful life'.

HOW TO DO IT

In *Salvage Style in Your Home* we have shown how quite simple salvaged items can be transformed into things of beauty. Not everything we have used for these projects will be available to you, but almost all the projects we have demonstrated can be adapted to use things you find, or may already own.

Most reclamation dealers are glad to give you the benefit of their knowledge – indeed it's sometimes hard to pull yourself away from an enthusiast in full verbal flow! Never be afraid to ask questions, for if he or she doesn't know the answer, then they generally know someone who does.

We list a number of the more common techniques used in the trade. Some you can undertake yourself, others will need to be done professionally.

LEFT

Taps and water pipes have been welded to a brass samovar, giving this bathroom in the Bristol restaurant Byzantium a feel of the exotic East.

BELOW

Three different reclaimed doors: the one on the left is one of a pair of outer French softwood louvre doors with fretted insert, original hinges, catches and paintwork, which was preserved with several applications of tung oil. The inner door on the right is glazed with an oak frame, and behind it is a pair of double doors with their original stained glass, used to hide kitchen paraphernalia.

AGEING METALS

It may be necessary to give new metals an impression of age. Virtually all metals tarnish over time, aged iron door furniture rusts, brass tarnishes and zinc dulls; when new replacements are used, their brashness can spoil the appeal of a project or repair. Whilst there are a number of commercially available 'cosmetic' treatments which can be bought in hobby and craft shops, often a simple process can accelerate natural ageing and the end result is more authentic.

ZINC

We use large quantities of perforated zinc for food larders made from old cupboards. New perforated zinc, available from most hardware stores or builders' merchants is bright and shiny and little resembles the fragile zinc used on old pieces of furniture.

It is a simple process to dissolve copper sulphate crystals (ordered from your chemist or pharmacist) in a little water and to wipe the solution over the new zinc with a soft cloth or sponge. The difference will be immediately apparent.

BRASS

Many designs of door furniture and handles have changed little over the years and new brass fittings are invaluable when their antique counterparts are not to be found.

For years we have kept a container of old and rather odiferous malt vinegar in our workshop – with an airtight lid! New brass fittings are dropped into the vinegar, left overnight and placed in the open air for a further twenty-four hours. The surface of the brass will have started to discolour and the shine dispelled. If this does not happen, it may

be that it has been sprayed with lacquer. Strip the lacquer with paint remover or caustic soda, wash and repeat the dipping process.

STEEL

Water is the age-old enemy of iron and steel, indeed vast sums of money are spent on preventing rust in industry and commerce. However, we frequently have to encourage steel to rust in order to match it to older pieces. Simply leave the steel out of doors and the weather will do your work for you. Rusting can be encouraged by heating the metal and then dousing it in water before leaving it for oxidation to take place; we find this process particularly useful for removing the paint from and ageing iron chain and black 'japanned' steel fittings.

CLEANING & POLISHING

Some materials need to be aged but in other circumstances the opposite is true and the same material must be cleaned or polished. The condition in which some salvaged materials can be found can discourage all but the most enthusiastic. Wood once used for cattle stalls encrusted with manure, beams of hardwood timber saturated with fungal attack, roll-top baths, chipped, stained and rusted; all can be rescued and restored to something approaching their former glory.

WOOD

Much hard and softwood salvaged timber is found heavily soiled or stained. Surface soiling can be removed with a pressure washer but remember the wood must be dry before being

re-used. It is important to dry wood under cover and stack it so that air can circulate around and in between the pieces.

Severely damaged or dirty timber can be shot or grit blasted, which will have the effect of removing the surface layer of softer material and grain as well as the soiling – a little dramatic but quite effective. A labour-intensive alternative is cleaning with a wire brush or a revolving wire or grit wheel.

All salvaged wood should be treated for rot, insect infestation and fungal attack before re-use, or the problem, if present, might spread to other timber. The UK company Cuprinol who assisted us with this book produce a range of effective wood treatment products as well as numerous colour finishes for interior wood and offer an invaluable advice service. (See the section 'Useful Addresses' at the end of this book.)

It is difficult to impart any polished finish to rough-cut or sawn timber but planed or smooth-surfaced timber can benefit from any of the various proprietary colour treatments or waxes which are available on the market. Choose the colour you use carefully as it is important to use the finish to enhance rather than mask the wood's natural grain.

For the enthusiast we recommend Frederick Oughton's book *The Complete Manual of Wood Finishing* which is highly informative about all things to do with the finishing and treatment of wood.

SLATE

We have used and discussed slate at length in various projects in this book. Slate is found in an almost bewildering range of subtle colours and is now imported into Europe and America from India, Mexico, China and Africa as well as many other countries for installation on roofs, floors, walls and work surfaces.

There are numerous proprietary slate polishes and sealants which any supplier will be all too happy to sell you, but it may well be worth considering the traditional Welsh custom of applying sour milk to slate floors to achieve a subtle finish. We have tried it, and it works. The fat present in the milk is absorbed by the slate whilst the drying liquid imparts a soft shine to its surface. A little smelly in application, the result is effective and can be easily removed with hot water and detergent.

It is worth passing on an idea from Hank Terry of Milo Design, a great enthusiast for using old roofing slates for flooring. Faced with the problem of what to do about the nail holes which mar so many reclaimed slates, he came up with the solution of filling the holes with molten lead once they had been laid. We have copied Hank's idea and found the best method of application is to use a blowtorch and lead soldering wire. Unwanted drips and splashes are easily removed and the end result is well worth the effort. On a cautionary note, always be careful to hold a blowtorch upright, wear protective glasses, gloves and clothing and never apply a blowtorch to a wet slate – or an explosion may result!

BRASS

Compare modern and antique brass and you will note a subtle difference in colour. Modern brass has more copper in its composition and professional restorers are careful to keep a stock of old brass for use when restoring antique pieces. Elbow grease and metal polish are the prerequisites for polishing brass – or call in the professionals. Paul Pitcher of Metal Arti-fix artifact and metal antique restorers swears that some brands of cola soft drinks and brown sauce are as effective at cleaning brass as most proprietary polishes; although we note he uses buffing machines and industrial compounds to clean and polish the range of keys, door furniture, old musical instruments and chandeliers which are his stock in trade.

Some abrasive polishing can be undertaken with electric hand tools, and buffing brushes and compounds can be obtained from industrial finishing and jewellery suppliers.

STEEL AND IRON

Elbow grease, wire brushes and metal polish are again the standard approach to polishing steel, although a buffing machine makes short work of a laborious job. Numerous fittings are made for electric hand tools which will help the amateur and are particularly useful for cleaning and polishing weathered and pitted iron. Black and Decker, one of the companies who assisted us in the production of this book, produce a useful range of electrical hand tools and fittings. See the section 'Useful Addresses' for details.

Cleaned and polished iron and steel should be protected with a coating of transparent furniture wax, but more effective is to spray with a proprietary metal lacquer.

To give a blackened appearance, wrought and cast iron can be given an authentic (and protective) finish with stove blacking paste. – a messy job but resulting in a finish far more attractive than paint can ever achieve.

BRICK AND TERRACOTTA

Old and stained bricks and terracotta can be cleaned with 'brick acid' sold by builders' merchants, or a solution of weak hydrochloric acid. Not a job to be undertaken lightly and one where it is essential that gloves, protective glasses and clothing as well as a face mask are worn. Seek professional advice before attempting such cleaning, or better still, leave it to the professionals.

Innumerable sealants and polishes formulated specially for terracotta floors are commercially available. Most seem perfectly adequate for the job and the best course of action is to seek a recommendation from your supplier or a previous user.

We have experimented very successfully with using bricks cut in half and laid as flooring. Old handmade bricks, when cut, can reveal a fascinating swirl of colours and pattern formed when the clay used to make them was hand cast into wooden moulds before firing. These patterns can be accentuated and the surface protected by an application of raw linseed oil; another messy but ultimately worthwhile job.

It may well be an apocryphal story, but we shall long treasure the recollection of an old builder who started his career as an apprentice during the First World War and told us of his experiences as a lad being made to clean the tar from the back of old inglenook fireplaces with a mixture of sand and dog faeces – apparently a very effective brick cleaner but not something we have tried.

REMOVING CHROME FROM TAPS

Many brass taps and bathroom fittings started
their life chrome plated. Chrome plating can be
removed by electrolysis in sulphuric acid but a
simpler process is by dipping in hydrochloric
acid, although this can result in the brass
pitting. Neither process should be attempted
by any other than the professional, properly
equipped and with the necessary experience.

PRESERVING TIMBER

Most forms of wood rot, worm and fungal
attack can be treated with commercial
products. All require that protective clothing is
worn and the user should always read and
follow the manufacturer's instructions. All
salvaged timber should be treated before use.

Treated timber which has softened can be
repaired with a proprietary wood hardener and
filled with wood filler to give many more years
of useful life. Cuprinol, who have assisted in
the production of this book, manufacture a
very effective hardener and a range of fillers.
See the section 'Useful Addresses' for details.

STRIPPING WOOD

Should you wish to remove paint from old
timber there are several choices. First however
you must be aware that old painted wood may
have been treated with lead-based paint. This
dangerous material is highly toxic – you must
take every precaution to prevent inhalation of
dust from it. Always wear a dust mask when
sanding, especially with power tools.

The first and most obvious method of paint
removal is sanding, either with any purpose-
made tools available or by hand. (We were
supplied with some very efficient power tools
by Black and Decker to help with the projects
for this book.) Sanding is time-consuming and
not only is it difficult to remove paint from
intricate areas, but also it may remove some of
the wood surface as well as the paint.

Heat stripping was once the usual method
of paint stripping available to the decorator;
paraffin heat guns have been replaced by gas
and electrical guns but both tend to scorch the
wood in all but the most experienced hands.

Chemical stripping is extremely effective and
particularly useful for stripping glued, fragile or
intricate objects. It is unpleasant, messy and
necessitates protective glasses and clothing,
but normally has less effect on the colour of
the wood than caustic stripping.

Caustic stripping is undertaken by
professional strippers (under Pine Stripping in
most directories). The results of immersion in a
hot caustic-filled tank are uniformly good on
most spirit-based paints. It is not normally
effective on water-based paints. The process
imparts colour to the dipped wood, especially if
the caustic has been in use for some time, and
can have the effect of loosening glued joints
and fixings. It is not advisable to strip
hardwoods in hot or cold caustic.

USEFUL ADDRESSES

TOOLS & SUPPLIES

BLACK AND DECKER
210 Bath Road, Slough
Buckinghamshire, SL1 3YD
Tel: 01753 511234
Fax: 01753 551155
website:
www.blackanddecker.com
Electrical and battery-powered
hand tools for the professional
and hobbyist.

SCREWFIX DIRECT
Mead Avenue, Houndstone
Business Park, Yeovil,
Somerset, BA22 8RT
Tel: 0500 41 41 41
Fax: 0800 056 22 56
email: online@screwfix.com
website: www.screwfix.com
Screws, nails, hardware and
tools; plumbing and electrical
supplies by mail order -
overnight.

TIMBER TREATMENT PRODUCTS

CUPRINOL LTD
Adderwell, Frome, Somerset,
BA11 1NL
Tel: 01373 475000
Fax: 01373 475050
Timber treatment products,
stains and colour washes for
internal and external use.
A useful advice line for
customer queries.

ARCHITECTS, DESIGNERS AND MANUFACTURERS

ADAMS AND SUTHERLAND
Studio 3c, Highgate Business
Centre, Greenwood Place,
London, NW5 1LB
Tel: 020 7267 1747
Fax: 020 7482 2359
email:
adams.sutherland@talk21.com
Architects sympathetic to the
use of reclaimed and salvaged
materials in new buildings,
renovations and environmental
improvements.

JOHN EDMONDS CABINET MAKERS
Buscott Farm, Station Road,
Ashcott, Bridgwater, Somerset,
TA7 9QP
Tel: 01458 210359
Fax: 01458 210096
email: enquiries@jecm.co.uk
website: www.jecm.co.uk
Cabinet makers, furniture
makers and restorers, building
restoration and designers
specialising in reclaimed
materials.

LAMBIEL ASSOCIATES
Queens Studios,
121 Salusbury Road,
London, NW6 6RG
Tel: 020 7624 1424
Fax: 020 7625 4310
email:
lambeil@compuserve.co.uk
Architects sympathetic to and
enthusiasts for the use of
reclaimed materials.

MILO DESIGN
34 Kings Parade Avenue,
Clifton, Bristol, BS8 2TS
Tel/Fax: 0117 973 7525
Mobile: 07977 489941/147101
Designers, shop, restaurant
and domestic interiors
designed and built, furniture
makers.

PORTER DESIGN
The Old Estate Yard,
Newton St Loe, Bath,
BA2 9BR
Tel: 01225 874250
Fax: 01225 874251
email:
sales@porter-design.com
website:
www.porter-design.com
Picture frames and mirrors, fine
art prints.

SOMERSET CREATIVE PRODUCTS
Laurel Farm, Westham,
Wedmore, Somerset,
BS28 4UZ
Tel: 01934 712416
Fax: 01934 712210
email:
somprods@globalnet.co.uk

Authors of *Salvage Style in Your
Home*; designers and makers of
furniture and accessories using
reclaimed materials.

WATSON BERTRAM & FELL
5 Gay Street, Bath, BA1 2PH
Tel: 01225 337273
Fax: 01225 448537
email:
wbfbath@compuserve.com
Architects specialising in work
on listed buildings or new
buildings in conservation areas
using reclaimed materials
wherever possible.

STAINED GLASS

DECORATIVE GLASS SUPPLIED LTD
Essex Mills, Essex Street,
Bradford, West Yorkshire,
BD4 7PG
Tel: 01274 773801
Fax: 01274 773802
email: dgsuk@aol.com
Stained and decorative glass
suppliers, tools, paints and
fusing supplies.

NEIL PHILLIPS STAINED GLASS
99 Portobello Road,
Notting Hill Gate, London,
W11 2QB
Tel: 020 7229 2113
Fax: 020 7229 1963
email: neil@neilphillips.co.uk
website:
www.neilphillips.co.uk
Leading specialists in the
conservation, restoration and
sale of antique stained glass -
SALVO Code dealer.

INFORMATION ON RECLAMATION & ARCHITECTURAL ANTIQUES DEALERS & SERVICES

SALVO
18 Ford Village,
Berwick-upon-Tweed,
Northumberland, TD15 2QG
Tel: 01890 820333

Fax: 01890 820499
email: salvoweb.com
website: www.salvoweb.com
Publishers of information on
architectural antiques,
reclamation dealers and
reclaimed building materials.
Originators of the SALVO Code
and the Salvo Code Dealer list.
The SALVO website links many
different reclamation dealers from
all over Britain and abroad.

RECLAMATION AND ARCHITECTURAL ANTIQUES DEALERS

ACE DEMOLITION & SALVAGE
Barrack Road, West Parley,
Ferndown, Dorset,
BH22 8UB
Tel: 01202 579222
Fax: 01202 582043
Mobile: 0589 478843
Reclaimed materials, timber,
bricks, tiles, RSJs, slates,
architectural items, recycled
concrete, sleepers, telegraph
poles - SALVO Code dealer.

ANDY THORNTON ARCHITECTURAL ANTIQUES LTD
Victoria Mills, Stainland Road,
Greetland, Halifax, West
Yorkshire, HX4 8AD
Tel: 01422 377314
Fax: 01422 310372
email: antiques@ataa.co.uk
website: ataa.co.uk
Architectural antiques and
decor; good quality interior
woodwork, fireplaces, panelling
and architectural features,
specialising in church interiors
for the refurbishment of pubs,
restaurants and hotels - SALVO
Code dealer.

ARCHITECTURAL ANTIQUES
351 King Street, Hammersmith,
London, W6 9NH
Tel/Fax: 020 8741 7883
Restoration and supply of
French fireplaces and mirrors.

ARTISAN OAK BUILDINGS
80 London Road, Teynham,
Kent, ME9 9QH
Tel: 01795 522121
Fax: 01795 520744
Structural and decorative old
oak beams and flooring –
SALVO Code dealer.

AU TEMPS PERDU
30 Midland Road, St Phillips,
Bristol, BS2 0JY
Tel: 0117 929 9143
Mobile: 0374 486648
Architectural antiques,
reclaimed building materials
and restoration 'Down to earth
materials at down to earth
prices' – SALVO Code dealer.

BRONDESBURY ARCHITECTURAL RECLAMATION
The Yard, 136 Willesden Lane,
Kilburn, London, NW6 7TE
Tel: 020 7328 0280
Fax: 020 7328 0280
Architectural antiques from
Georgian to Edwardian periods,
doors, baths, fireplaces, old
radiators and heat output
sheets – SALVO Code dealer.

COUNTRY BROCANTE
Fir Tree Farm, Godney,
Somerset, BA5 1RZ
Tel/Fax: 01458 833052
Mobile: 07970 719708
email: ovel@compuserve.com
French antique country
furniture and artifacts,
chandeliers and mirrors.

COUNTRY OAK
Little Washbrook Farm,
Brighton Road, Hurstpierpoint,
West Sussex, BN6 9EF
Tel/Fax: 01273 833869
Mobile: 0402 974418
Specialists in old French and
English oak beams and flooring,
also fire surrounds, tiles and
flagstones – SALVO Code
dealer.

DORSET RECLAMATION
The Reclamation Yard,
Cow Drove, Bere Regis,
Dorset, BH20 7JZ

Tel: 01929 472200
Fax: 01929 472292
email:
tessa@dorsetrec.u-net.com
Reclaimed traditional building
materials, architectural
antiques, bathroom, lighting and
fireplace showrooms - SALVO
Code dealer.

**DRUMMONDS
ARCHITECTURAL ANTIQUES**
The Kirkpatrick Buildings,
25 London Road, Hindhead,
Surrey, GU26 6AB
Tel: 01428 609444
Fax: 01428 609445
email:
info@drummonds-arch.co.uk
website:
www.drummonds-arch.co.uk
Antique garden, architectural
and bathroom items - SALVO
Code dealer.

**EASY – EDINBURGH
ARCHITECTURAL SALVAGE**
Unit 6, Couper Street, Leith,
Edinburgh, EH6 6HH
Tel: 0131 554 7077
Fax: 0131 554 3070
email:
enquiries@easy-arch-salv.co.uk
website:
www.easy-arch-salv.co.uk
Architectural antiques, fixtures
and fittings, fireplaces all
under one roof - SALVO
Code dealer.

FROME RECLAMATION
Station Approach, Wallbridge,
Frome, Somerset, BA11 1RE
Tel: 01373 463919
Fax: 01373 453122
Mobile: 0836 277507
Pine doors, fireplaces, slates,
tiles, beams, flooring, antique
stoneware, furniture, bygones
etc. - SALVO Code dealer.

**JAT ENVIRONMENTAL
RECLAMATION**
The Barn, Lower Littleton Farm,
Winford Road, Chew Magna,
Bristol, BS40 8HJ
Tel: 01275 333589
Fax: 01275 474680
Mobile: 0966 543838

Reclaimed stone, roof and
ridge tiles, softwood timber,
bricks and beams - SALVO
Code dealer.

LASSCo
St Michaels Church, Mark
Street, London, EC2A 4ER
Tel: 020 7749 9944
Fax: 020 7749 9941
email:
st.michaels@lassco.co.uk
website: www.lassco.co.uk
The largest architectural
salvage company with five
depots in London; lighting,
stained glass, chimney pieces,
radiators, bathrooms, kitchens,
pews, church and pub furniture
oak, pine and teak flooring etc.
- SALVO Code dealer.

PEW CORNER
Artington Manor Farm,
Old Portsmouth Road,
Guildford, Surrey, GU3 1HP
Tel: 01483 533337
Fax: 01483 535554
email:
pewcorner@pewcorner.co.uk
website:
www.pewcorner.co.uk
Absolutely everything and
anything from the interiors of
churches; handmade furniture
crafted from reclaimed timber -
SALVO Code dealer.

RETROUVIUS
32 York House, Upper
Montagu Street, London,
W1H 1FR
Tel: 020 7724 3387
Fax: 020 7402 6826
Mobile: 0378 210855
Architect proprietors working
with salvaged materials in
contemporary settings.
Bridging the gap between
construction and destruction;
dismantled building components
for reuse in interiors and
exteriors – SALVO Code dealer.

**ROBERT MILLS
RECLAMATION**
Narroways Road, Eastville,
Bristol, BS2 9XB
Tel: 0117 955 6542

Fax: 0117 955 8146
email:
robert.mills.ltd@dial.pipex.com
Specialist in gothic architectural
antiques including paneling,
stained glass and church fittings
for pubs, restaurants and private
houses - SALVO Code dealer.

TALISMAN
The Old Brewery, Wyke,
Gillingham, Dorset, SP8 4NW
Tel: 01747 824423/824222
Fax: 01747 823544
email:
talisman@globalnet.co.uk
Architectural antiques for
interiors and gardens.

WALCOT RECLAMATION LTD
The Depot, Riverside Business
Park, Lower Bristol Road,
Bath, BA2 3PQ
Tel: 01225 335532
Fax: 01225 484317
Old-established reclamation
yard specialising in architectural
antiques, reclaimed building
materials, bathroom fittings etc.

WELLS RECLAMATION
The Old Cider Farm, Coxley,
Wells, Somerset, BA5 1RQ
Tel: 01749 677087
Fax: 01749 671089
email:
enquiries@wellsreclamation.com
Comprehensive stock of
architectural antiques and
reclaimed traditional building
materials.

WESTLAND & COMPANY
St Michael's Church, Mark
Street, London, EC4A 4ER
Tel: 020 7729 3620
Fax: 020 7729 3620
email:
westland@westland.co.uk
website: www.westland.co.uk
Antique chimney pieces, fine
grates, architectural elements,
paneling, paintings and furniture.

**WILSONS CONSERVATION
BUILDING PRODUCTS**
123 Hillsborough Road,
Dromore, Co. Down, Northern
Ireland, BT25 1QW

Tel: 01846 692304
Fax: 01846 698322
email: rosyw@enterprise.net
Architectural antiques and
reclaimed materials. Flooring,
beams and architectural items;
cast iron and metalwork; clay
and stone bricks, floor tiles, wall
capping, setts and cobbles,
flagstones etc.

METAL RESTORATION & SUPPLIES

**BRISTOL RESTORATION
WORKSHOPS**
8 Devon Road, Easton, Bristol,
BS5 9AE
Tel/Fax: 0117 954 2114
Restoration of metalware and
furniture, dismantling, recasting,
remaking of missing pieces,
rebuilding, polishing, recolouring
and lacquering.

CHARTERBRAE LTD
Coneygre Industrial Estate,
Tipton, West Midlands,
DY4 8XP
Tel: 0121 520 5353
Fax: 0121 522 2018
Metal bed frames and fittings.

LAMPARTS
The Square, Ramsbury,
Wiltshire, SN8 2PA
Tel: 01672 520454
Fax: 01672 520560
email: lampartsltd.co.uk
Shades, fittings, glass drops,
wicks for oil lamps, fittings to
convert old gas lamps to
electricity, candle drops, glass
mantles etc.

METAL ARTI-FIX
35 Manor Road, Bishopston,
Bristol, BS7 8PZ
Tel: 0117 944 5491
Mobile: 0771 559 4947
Antique and artifact restorers
specialising in metal items,
works in brass, lead, copper,
steel and glass.

ARTISTS AND CRAFTSPEOPLE

PAUL ANDERSON
104 West Street, Hartland,
Devon
Tel: 01237 441645
Maker of primitve furniture
crafted from old oak or elm
joists, gates and fences which
revels in its textures, rich colours
and surface blemishes.

CANDACE BAHOUTH
The Old Ebenezer Chapel,
Pilton, Somerset
Tel: 01749 890433
Mosaic artist working in wide
variety of reclaimed materials.

**MADELAINE BOULESTEIX
CHANDELIERS**
2 Carlton Mansions,
387 Coldharbour Lane,
London, SW9 8QD
Tel: 020 7737 8171
Handmade recycled electrical
and candle-lit chandeliers.

**RICHARD WALLACE and
CORRINNA SARGOOD**
17 Paul Street, Frome,
Somerset, BA11 1DT
Tel: 01373 473970
Furniture maker and artist.

GOVERNMENT SURPLUS STORE

HARPER'S BAZAAR
263 Worcester Road, Malvern
Link, Malvern, Worcestershire,
WR14 1AA
Tel: 01684 568723
Fax: 01905 612837
Government surplus suppliers;
office and domestic furniture,
garden and camping supplies,
storage, beds, chairs etc.

CANADA

ALL AROUND DEMOLITION CO. LTD.
4912 Still Creek Avenue,
Burnaby, British Columbia,
V1X 2C1
Tel: + 1 604 299 2967
Fax: + 1 604 299 1383

HAPPY HARRY'S USED BUILDING MATERIALS
4128 South Service Road,
Burlington, Ontario, L71 4X5
Tel: + 1 905 631 0990
Fax: + 1 905 631 0991
website: www.happyharry.com
Salvaged doors, windows, plumbing supplies, staircases, spindles, architectural glass and doors, blocks and bricks.

HAPPY HARRY'S USED BUILDING MATERIALS
5044 45th Street,
Red Deer, Alberta, T4N 1K9
Tel: + 1 403 343 1818
website: www.happyharry.com
Demolition recycling. Mainly salvaged windows and doors.

HAPPY HARRY'S USED BUILDING MATERIALS
20 Bulmer Lane, Sackville
New Brunswick, E4L 3R4
Tel: + 1 506 364 0803
Fax: + 1 506 198 5364
email:
gbeland@mailserv.mta.ca
website: www.happyharry.com
New, second and reclamation building materials.

HAPPY HARRY'S USED BUILDING MATERIALS
140 Caledonia Road,
Caledonia Industrial Park,
Moncton, New Brunswick,
E4L 3R4
Tel/fax: + 1 506 855 7999
email:
gbeland@mailserv.mta.ca
website: www.happyharry.com
Salvaged building materials.

HAPPY HARRY'S USED BUILDING MATERIALS
46 Wright Avenue,
Burnside Industrial Park,
Dartmouth, Nova Scotia,
B3B 1G6
Tel: + 1 902 468 2319
Fax: + 1 902 468 3666
Windows, doors and plumbing particularly.

MIKE'S SALVAGE
Penetanguishene, Ontario,
L9M 1R
Tel: + 1 705 533 4457
email: mikev@csolve.net
Lumber, doors, windows, trim, plumbing, electrical fixtures.

UNIQUITIES ARCHITECTURAL ANTIQUES
940 2nd Avenue NW,
Calgary, Alberta, T2N 0E6
Tel: + 1 403 228 9221
Fax: + 1 403 283 9226
email: shantzj@cadvision.com

AUSTRALIA

AUSTRALIAN ARCHITECTURAL HARDWOODS
45-47 South Street, Kempsey
Tel: + 61 2 6562 2788
Reclaimed timber including flooring and sections.

INTEXT PACIFIC PTY LTD
13 St John's Parade, Kew,
Victoria 3101
Tel: + 61 3 9853 0364
Fax: +61 3 9853 3302
email: intex@bigpond.net.au
website:
www.intexpacific.com
Suppliers of natural landscape and garden materials including railway sleepers and large selection old bricks.

OLD RED BRICK COMPANY
16 William Street,
Beverley, South Australia
Tel: + 61 8 8347 2419
Fax: + 61 8 8347 2144
Salvaged doors, windows, bricks and timber.

QUALITY RECYCLED DEMOLITIONS
34 Woodfield Boulevard,
Caringbah 2229,
Sydney, NSW
Tel: + 61 2 9542 7203
Fax: + 61 2 9531 5762
Custom-make a huge array of items (baths, doors, windowframes etc.) with a number of materials including timber and bricks.

SECOND HAND BUILDING CENTRE
432B West Botany Street
Rockdale, NSW 2216
Tel: + 61 2 9567 1322
Fax: + 61 2 9597 1782
email: info@shbc.com.au
website: www.shbc.com.au
Complete range of reclaimed timber, building materials, hardware, baths and sanitary fittings and architectural antiques.

SELECT SALVAGE
76 Smith Street,
Kensington, Victoria
Tel: + 61 3 9376 2543
Showroom open Mon–Sat,
10am–4pm.

THE SYDNEY SECONDHAND SANDSTONE COMPANY
Brookvale, Sydney
Tel/Fax: + 61 2 9905 7151
Mobile: 0408 259155
Based in Sydney, which was built on sandstone, this company buys and preserves old sandstone which they sell on to stone-masons, builders and homeowners.

VIC PARK SALVAGE
39 Briggs Street,
Welshpool, WA
Tel: + 61 9472 3316
Fax: + 61 9470 4615
Architectural antiques, windows, doors, de-nailed timber, flooring and lots more.

NEW ZEALAND

EASTWOOD RECYCLED BUILDING SUPPLIES
171 Kaikorai Valley Road,
Dunedin
Tel: + 64 3 476 7868

HERITAGE 100% RECYCLED
61 Ward Street, Dunedin,
South Island
Tel/Fax: + 64 3 474 9405
Bricks, gates, doors, paving, salvaged hardwood, sleepers etc.

KAMAPAT NEW AND RECYCLED TIMBER
7 Matai Street, Stoke Nelson
South Island
Tel: + 64 3 547 8158
Fax: + 64 3 547 8128
email: KAPAMAK@xtra.co.nz
website:
www.skyboom/realcrafty.co.nz
(look under recycled timber for details)
They sell among other things products made from 100% pure New Zealand timber.

MANAWATU HOUSE PARTS
102 Armstrong House,
Palmerston North
Tel: + 64 6 355 0043

PUMP HOUSE SALVAGE YARD
Cnr Tuan & Mathesons Road,
Linwood, Christchurch
Tel: + 64 3 389 6638

THE RENOVATOR'S CENTRE
40 Perry Street, Masterton,
North Island
Tel/Fax: + 64 6 378 8422
Kitchens, bathrooms. doors, windows etc. Furniture, French doors and windows made from recycled timber.

SOUTHERN RECYCLED TIMBER
380 Waterloo Road,
Christchurch
Tel: + 64 3 349 2534

EIRE

THE ORIGINAL ARCHITECTURAL SALVAGE COMPANY
South Gloucester Street,
Dublin 2
Tel: + 353 1 677 3557
Fax: + 353 1 677 3318
email:
info@architecturalclassics.com
website:
www.architecturalclassics.com
Sanitary ware, bathroom fittings, antique lighting, door furniture, garden statuary, chimney pieces, fireplace accessories and lots more.

INDEX

ACKNOWLEDGMENTS

This full-length mirror demonstrates an imaginative use of weathered timber from a disused farm gate. Note the clever use of the original gate hinges and the bolts at the bottom of the mirror which conceal balancing weights behind.

Our thanks to Kyle Cathie Publishers, editors **Kate Oldfield** and **Helen Woodhall**, our photographer **Tim Winter** and his assistant **Jo Fairclough**

Our thanks also to the companies who generously helped us with equipment, materials and advice:

Black and Decker
Hand and power tools for the professional and handyman
Cuprinol Ltd
Timber treatment products and decorative colour stains and finishes.
Screwfix Direct
Hardware and tools by mail order – overnight.

Also to all those who kindly allowed us to photograph their homes and business premises.

Angela Coombes and
Michael Hewitt
Peter and **Sarah Fineman**
Peter Watson and
Jacqui Spencer
Elizabeth and **Crispin Deacon**
Saltmoor House, Saltmoor, Burrowbridge, Somerset TA7 0RL Tel. 01823 698092. Caterers, who also offer a prestigious Bed and Breakfast service
Arne Ringner proprietor Byzantium restaurant, 2 Portwall Lane, Bristol, BS1 6NB. Tel. 0117 922 1883

Fax. 0117 922 1886
email info@byzantium.co.uk
website www.byzantium.co.uk
Roger and **Monty Saul**
Charlton House Hotel, Shepton Mallet, Somerset BA4 4PR
Tel. 01749 342008,
Fax. 01749 346362,
email reservations-charltonhouse@btinternet.com,
website www.mulberry-england.co.uk

Thanks to Bob Whitfield for his shots of the interior of the home of Hank and Sophia Terry (the owners of Milo Design).

And to the following people whose addresses can be found in our 'Useful Addresses' section.

Candace Bahouth: mosaic artist;
Pete Chapman and **Jeff Blagdon**: Au Temps Perdu; **Haydn Davies**: Wells Reclamation; **John Edmonds**: John Edmonds Cabinet Makers; **Lawrence Harper**: Harper's Bazaar; **Steve Horler**: Frome Reclamation; **Thornton Kay** and **Hazel Matravers**: SALVO; **Robert Mills**: Robert Mills Reclamation; **Tim** and **Nicky Ovel**: Country Brocante; **Henry** and **Mary Porter**: Porter Design; **Hank** and **Sophia Terry**: Milo Design; **John** and **Mike Tyler**: JAT Reclamation; **Richard Wallace** and **Corrinna Sargood**: furniture maker and artist; **Mark Watson** of Watson Bertram and Fell: architects